Potterton Books

With the co-operation
of Maria Jedding-Gesterling

Edmund Launert

Perfume and Pomanders

From the Schwarzkopf Collection
and European Museums

Scent and Scent Bottles

Potterton Books

To Page 2:
Fig. 1 Double-walled bottle in "ivory" porcelain. Outer wall pierced in a flower and foliage pattern. Acanthus leaves on the shoulder, highlighted in gold. England, Royal Worcester or Grainger, c. 1875. H. 85 mm. P. London

First published 1985 by Georg D. W. Callwey GmbH & Co., Munich, under the title: "Parfüm und Flakons"

Translated from the German by
JEAN M. LAUNERT

Printed in Germany 1987
ISBN 1 870599 01 2

Scent containers

Only a small part of this book is concerned with the perfume containers of ancient civilisations, and that can only be a brief rather than a detailed survey. The emphasis is mainly on European scent bottles from mediaeval to modern times. The specimens from the classical world which are illustrated come from the Schwarzkopf collection, with additional material from the British Museum. In actual fact the quantity of examples which have survived from the ancient world is enormous, as can easily be ascertained by a visit to the great museums, especially the British Museum, as already mentioned, and the Musée du Louvre. These vessels merit a volume of their own which would also deal with the hygiene and art of cosmetics of their period.

The oldest scent containers we know are from the Eastern Mediterranean, the acknowledged cradle of our civilisation. The earliest evidence of the use of perfumes in both sacred and profane activities comes from Ancient Egypt, as do in consequence the first vessels designed to keep these precious substances. The choice of materials was limited: most common is terracotta, and it remained so throughout the Greek and Early Roman periods. Semi-precious metal was of minor importance only. The use of glass thus was a later Egyptian development, increasing in favour throughout succeeding centuries and eventually supplanting terracotta.

By far the largest category of terracotta containers were anthropomorphic in character, followed by actual animal shapes, notably the many representations of the fish. The straightforward vase shape is relatively rare. The head of a sphinx and that of a warrior are among the earliest examples from the 6th century in the British Museum collection. Judging by their decoration, many were made in imitation of semi-precious stone. Along with geometrical shapes and symbols, the world of the gods in the form of, for example, representations of Isis and Amun-Re, the sun god, is frequently drawn upon. It is hard to say whether the use of terracotta spread from Ancient Egypt to other Mediterranean lands and the Near East or, as is more likely, was developed independently there. A contributing factor was the continuous trade between the merchants of the Nile and other neighbouring regions of the Mediterranean. In any case, terracotta pottery reached its zenith in Classical Greece as is also clearly shown by the small examples of this art in Ill. (11–17). No other people depicted its daily life and culture on its pottery to the same extent as the Greeks – one need only consider the tremendous number of urns and vases still extant. The decoration on these objects tells us more about their customs, religion and life from the cradle to the grave than do their written history and poetry. Their flacons for ointments and scented oils again show mainly anthropomorphic forms: female and warrior heads, sirens and goddesses. Among the animal inspired flacons we frequently find hedgehogs, ducks, bulls' and rams' heads, and there are isolated examples of a hare and a sitting ape. In Volci in Etruria a bottle in the form of a Gorgon's head was excavated. A surprisingly frequent motif is the sandalled foot in

Fig. 2   Scent bottles in the form of fabulous creatures (probably pigs). Roman, 3–4th Ct. AD. RGM

various designs and sizes. As for vase shapes, the aryballos is almost exclusively favoured: a particularly beautiful piece is decorated with a hunting scene around the somewhat widened upper rim. The excavations in Camirus on Rhodes were a rich source for our museums, interesting pieces also came to light on Samos and in Milet.

The origins of glass manufacture are shrouded in mystery. Glass was most probably discovered independently in different regions – certainly this is the case in the Near East. Glass vessels from Egypt have been known since the 15th century B. C. Very early vessels were cut from a block of solid glass and subsequently polished. Ointment pots, alabasters and flacons from the period after 8 B.C. made in this way are to be found, if not in great quantities, in several collections. Another technique involved glass being moulded and cut and polished after cooling. For the historian of scent containers another technique is of prime importance, because it accounts for hundreds if not thousands of examples. They are present, and there are even fakes of them, in almost every collection. They were manufactured within a period of about 800 years from roughly the 7th century B.C. and hardly vary from a basic form. Almost all of them show coloured threads or stripes in wavy or zig-zag lines fused into the body of the vessel (Ill. 1). They were known under the collective term of sand core vessels because it was believed they were formed round a core of hardened sand. Today it is assumed instead that this core consisted of a mixture of mud, dung and straw. The Egyptian origin of these aesthetically pleasing containers is also questioned nowadays, since hardly any have been found in Egypt itself.

The most revolutionary advance in the field of glass technology was the invention of the glassblower's pipe in Sidon on the coast of Syria, not long after the birth of Christ. Within a short time hollow glasses were being manufactured, not only in Sidon and Alexandria, but in the farthest outposts of the Roman Empire, even in southern England. One of the most important glass making centres north of the Alps was Cologne, where, as well as a great number of hollow glasses and other items, fine flacons have been brought to light through excavation (Fig. 3). Among the flacons of the Roman period the mould blown examples outnumber the free-blown. Many are imitative of terracotta or bronze artefacts. Anthropomorphic designs are once more to the fore (Ill. 18), then there are also animals (Fig. 2), shells and fruits, especially grapes. As in all other cultures the fish shape is present in all its forms and variations (Fig. 4, 41).

After the fall of the Roman Empire and the Roman retreat a cultural darkness fell over Europe, which did not exempt the glass industry. Several centuries were to pass before it was revived in Venice.

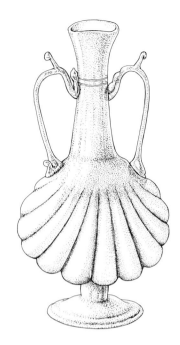

Fig. 3 Shell shaped scent bottle on round foot with applied handles. Iridescent glass. Rheno-Roman, 3–4th Ct. AD. Drawn from a piece in the RGM.

Fig. 4 Scent bottles in the form of fishes. Colourless glass with olive green details. Roman, 3–4th Ct. AD. RGM

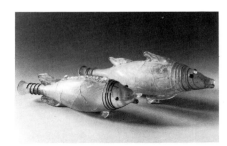

The sweetening of the atmosphere by burning aromatic substances goes far back in history and is common to all cultures. It is the oldest method of perfuming: per fumum (through smoke) is the Latin origin of the word perfume.

The perfuming of the air per se, its pleasurable effect and stimulation of the olfactory sense was of only secondary importance. Whether or not the practice arose as a manner of disguising the smell of decomposition at funeral rites is open to question. Originally incense was an integral part of religious ritual; it projected animalistic and cosmic concepts.

The smoke, invading the sense of smell and visible to the eye, had a symbolic meaning. It stood for purification, accompanying and guiding the prayers of the faithful up to heaven; it seemed like the soul as it left the body and was the transcendental made manifest, the way to God. Perfume became synonymous with life and wellbeing and was seen as an offering to the deity.

But incense had in most religions another, one might say practical, raison d'être: by heightening his senses it increased the capacity of the worshipper to meditate and concentrate on prayer. Its narcotic effect, which in some religious cults was acceptable as a manner of achieving the state of ecstasy, cannot be ignored.

Murals from pre-hellenistic Egypt show figures, arms outstretched, holding incense dishes; the suppliants are asking the god to draw the soul to himself with the smoke. They offer him perfumed resins at sunrise, myrrh at high noon and the legendary perfume Kyphi at nightfall. Incense was also burnt in flat, open, golden dishes in front of the temple. There is a representation of Thotmes IV burning incense on a granite slab on the breast of the Sphinx.

Incense was burnt in China both in the temple and in the home in the course of daily religious ceremony. There are bronze burners dating from the Chou period (c 1120–221 B.C.). In the Metropolitan Museum of Art in New York one may admire a three-legged censer richly decorated with bird motifs which came from the western Chou Dynasty (1027–771 B.C.). The T'ang Dynasty (618–906 A.D.) has provided gilded pierced containers which were held in the hand during votive ceremonies. In the huge collections of the museum in Chang there is a finely worked, spherical incense container in pierced gold, probably, in view of its chain, intended for wearing round the neck. Inside, and this is what makes it especially interesting, is a small dish for the burning of incense, suspended in such a way as to retain a horizontal position however the censer is swung, thereby avoiding spillage of the incense. This device is in accordance with the so-called Cardanic principle, which must therefore have been known to the Chinese long before its discovery in Europe. This censer, according to a Chinese documentary film shown in Paris, is also of the T'ang period.

A perfect specimen of a perfume burner in white glazed porcelain excavated in Ting-hsien in 1969 would seem to anticipate its 18th century European counterpart. It sits on five supporting columns in the form of fantasy creatures and is provided with a lid pierced with a few holes. It is given a Sung Dynasty (960–1279 A.D.) attribution.

In Japanese culture the Kodan, a vessel with pierced lid, is used in both Buddhist and Shinto rituals. It was customary to burn sticks impregnated with incense at the graves of the Samurai. The burners often have animal shapes. The Museum für Kunst und Gewerbe in Hamburg has some showing ornithological inspiration in the form of cranes. It is interesting in this connection to note that a chronicler of the 13th century wrote of the existence of two silver incense burners in the form of lifesize birds in the treasury of Mainz Cathedral.

India surpasses all other lands with its vast and varied perfume cult. From time immemorial, Hindus and more particularly Muslims have burned incense, indeed most liberally, at religious ceremonies such as circumcision, marriage and cremation. One thousand five hundred years before Christ the Verdas were burning aromatic substances to accompany their prayers and to emphasise their respect, devotion and thankfulness to the deity. The burning of perfume had at the same time a profane use. Apart from the aromatic resins which had been imported from Arabia and the surrounding islands from early times, local products, mainly sandalwood and cassia, were the main ingredients of Indian incense. Even today incense offerings are burnt on the temple steps, usually before daybreak. In the cult of Shiva priests make daily offerings of incense before the stone in Orissa which represents the deity, and incense plays a great part in the religion of Buddhists and other sects in Asian countries. Similarly it has been offered before Buddha figures in the temples of Tibet and the monasteries of the Lamas since ancient times.

The custom is by no means restricted to the Old World. In pre-Columbian Mexico and Peru both golden dishes and heated uncovered terracotta pots were strewn with, mainly, copal (Hymenae species) and herbs, thereby sending the crowd of worshippers into narcotic transports. Their most important god, Quetzalcóatl, was honoured four times a day with incense offerings. There are several references to the use of incense by the Jews in the Bible. According to the Jewish doctor Maimonides, aromatic substances were burnt in order to mask the stench incurred during the burning of sacrificial animals. In the later period of the Temple in Jerusalem the production of incense was in the hands of a priest family by the name of Euthynos and the formula was their guarded secret. In an earlier period there were votive burnings in honour of the Torah. In the cabbala the four ingredients of the substance used are given: Balsam, the opercula of marine molluscs (mainly Murex), Galbanum and incense. These four basic materials of biblical times stood for the four elements, namely water, earth, air and fire. In Christian adaptation they represent the four forms of prayer (Beseeching, Intercession, Praise and Thanks) or the four manners of comportment for the person at prayer (Humility, Belief, Love, Hope). The burning of incense accompanied the worship of the early Christians, the custom having been adopted from the Romans. It is noteworthy that Saint Augustine (354–430), when banning all pleasures of the flesh, exempted the enjoyment of pleasant scents. Constantine the Great is said to have provided scented oils for burning on Rome's altars. He presented the church of St. John Lateran with several incense containers, presumably intended for diffusing scents. Liturgical significance was accorded to incense only from the 7th century when it was burned in honour of bishops and the Holy Scripture. From the 13th century onwards vessels for incense were part and parcel of the furniture of every church, as the inventories prove. The essential components of incense were olibanum (Frankincense), benzoin (gum benjamin) amd Labdanum – materials which were imported from Alexandria, Byzantium, and also Cyprus. As the accounts of the great cathedrals show, incense henceforth played a great part in church liturgy and the custom has been maintained in the Roman Catholic Church and to an even greater degree in the orthodox churches of the East. Only in the churches of Northern Europe did the custom, like so much else, come to an end as a result of the Reformation. An exceptional re-adoption was that of the High Anglican Church in the 19th century when the ancient tradition of the swung censer, its chains clinking, was re-introduced. During the earliest times of its use, incense was strewn on glowing coals in open burners. Such burners were, of course, static and, even when provided with handles, the degree to which they could be moved by the priest celebrating the religious office was limited. In the 9th century, with the design of the swinging incense burner – the turibulum, thymaterrium or incensorium, to give it its various names – the pierced lid was a natural addition. The swinging of the censer seems to have had no liturgical significance, merely serving to fan the coals and send the wafts of incense into the body of the church.

Down the centuries the censer has been the object of the craftsman's finest efforts in bronze, silver and gold. Usually architectural in style, it has always reflected the given period, from the romanesque to the present day. Although showing great variations of style its basic form remains the same. It consits of a bowl-like container for the charcoal, to which usually three chains are attached, surmounted by an artistically-pierced cover loosely secured by them, and with a central chain which allows the cover to move upwards (Ill. 24).

The censers illustrated here represent a fraction of the hundreds that exist. The censers of the Gothic period merit a study in themselves, particularly the Italian and Spanish ones, and the same may be said of their iconography. Angels holding censers are a common theme in both painting and sculpture and bear witness to the liturgical significance of the practice down the

Fig. 5 One of a pair of carved early baroque angels with censer. Shrine of Tuntenhausen (Upper Bavaria). Gilt wood, c. 1630.

centuries. Very impressive, if not easily noticed, is such a representation in the stained glass windows of the cathedral of Freiburg im Breisgau (Fig. 6).

For the enthusiast Bavaria is a real Aladdin's cave; from the many examples suffice it to mention a few: a censer holding angel, one of 12 stone reliefs dating from the 12th century over the portal of the church of St. Andreas in Bad Gögging, Lower Bavaria (This figure had also been identified as one of the wise virgins bearing a lamp, but the nature of this vessel hanging on chains makes this interpretation unlikely). Also in Lower Bavaria, a fine specimen on the high altar of the Convent church of Osterhofen-Altenmarkt, decorated by the Asam brothers; two angels flanking the tabernacle in the church of St. Anna im Lehel (Munich), these by Johann Baptist Straub; a kneeling angel of fervent mien in the Convent church in Weyarn by Ignaz Gunther; a similar angel by the same master dating from 1767 on the high altar in the late baroque church of St. Michael in Berg am Laim, also in Munich; a similar angel can just be made out on the ceiling in the magnificent church by the Asam brothers in the Sendlingerstrasse. A representation of a particular kind may be seen in the protestant church of St. Ulrich in Augsburg. In Matthias Lotter's stucco ceiling two censers linked by ribbons swing among the rocaille ornamentation, side by side with figures of the apostles, the Virgin Mary and many symbols of the Christian faith.

Fig. 6 Angel with censer. From a stained glass window (the so-called "Schneiderfenster") in Freiburg Cathedral (Germany), c. 1320. From Corpus Vitrearum Medii Aevi (R. Wohlrabe)

Apart from the censers attached to chains there were many others which served the same purpose. Mention has already been made of the two silver ornithological examples in the form of cranes in the Mainz Cathedral Treasury, so designed that the smoke issues from their bills. They were intended to stand on each side of the altar. There are reports of heads (capita) from the mouths of which smoke would issue and it is assumed that some aquamaniles were used to the same effect.

Fig. 7 The large censer (el butafumeiro) in the Cathedral of Santiago de Compostela. H. (inc. chain) 180 cm

The highpoint of the incense cult may be witnessed in Spain, in the church of Santiago de Compostela. The largest censer in the world suspended from a rope as thick as one's arm is set in motion by three red garbed servers, high above the crowd of pilgrims from all over Europe to St. James's shrine, a spectacular effect which could not be bettered by the most imaginative metteur-en-scène at the opera (Fig. 7).

The precious nature of incense and its sacred intention is reflected in the containers made for it. Set rules of worship ordain that incense be used at certain points in the Mass; the priest must have it readily at hand at the right moment. The containers, known as *acerra* or *busta*, took on different forms and it is probable that in the early Middle Ages the Pyxis, generally used for the keeping of the consecrated wafer, also safeguarded the incense. After the 13th century the navicula, a boat-shaped vessel, appears. A particularly beautiful gilt one, remarkable for its simplicity, each end ornamented with a crowned ram's head, may be seen in the Victoria and Albert Museum in London. It dates from the 14th century and comes from Ramsey Abbey, thereby explaining the ram's heads (Ramsey: ram) and is one of the noblest pieces of sacred metal-work of this period (Ill. 24).

The priest celebrating Mass would take incense on an incense spoon from the covered container and strew it on the glowing charcoal of the turribulum. Spoons for this purpose were also artistically wrought; very fine examples are to be found in the treasuries of most cathedrals. There is a famous one of Flemish origin, decorated with a figure of St. Catherine, in the Victoria and Albert Museum.

It is only a small step from the use of incense as a spiritual uplift in religious worship to its use in warding off evil spirits, disease and any other bringer of misfortune. Three thousand years ago the people of Babylon and Assyria tried to defeat the demons who were thought to bring sickness with a ritual involving incense burning and chanting. Hippocrates considered scents to be medically effective and suggested that the plague might be driven from Athens with the help of aromatic fires. His teaching dominated medical thinking throughout the Middle Ages and even in the 18th century people still believed in the therapeutic powers of scent, and the scent did not necessarily have to be of an agreeable sort. Scented substances were not only breathed in but applied to anus and vagina. Particularly when plague was rife, the burning of aromatic substances took place in an effort to dispel the "aura" of the disease. Saltpetre, sulphur, tar, and incense were used and particularly penetrating fumes were obtained by burning leather, horn and gunpowder. During the plague in London in 1563 each householder was obliged to ignite a large pile of wood three times a week and during the Great Plague in the following century hundreds of fires were kept burning night after night by night watchmen. People's houses were fumigated as a precaution or in an attempt to rid them of plague. To carry this out aromatic substances were placed on heated tiles – sometimes with vinegar – or they were put into earthenware perfume burners (Ill. 25, 26). In the Schweizerisches Pharmaziehistorisches Museum in Basle there is an interesting four-legged iron perfume burner dating from the 17th century. A chronicler relates that during the Great Plague of 1665 the deanery of St. Paul's was fumigated weekly by burning olibanum, sulphur, hops and pepper, an undertaking which can by no means have been cheap. In the homes of the nobility and wealthier citizens aromatic substances were heated in so-called "cassolettes", metal boxes with punctured lids which were placed on or near the fire. This custom survived the time of the plague: cassolettes and similar containers were forerunners of perfume burners. Tobacco was also used as an anti-plague agent in the 17th century. At that time it was still a luxury item, a fact that can be ascertained from the smallness of the pipe bowls used. Women and indeed children were encouraged to smoke. One Dr. Atkinson recommended that pulverised Angelica root be softened for several days in vinegar and the resulting concoction heated in a pan for the purpose of inhaling or for the decontamination of clothes. Plague doctors in France advised not only fumigation with aromatic herbs and with vinegar poured on red hot metal, and even arsenic, but also the carrying of smelling cushions (see also page 31) filled with herbs, mainly of the labiate family (Labiatae), and orange and lemon peel, as well as bay leaves and cloves. Angelica root is also a feature in their recipes.

PERFUME BURNERS

It would be a mistake to think of perfume only as an adjunct to religious worship or as a means of combatting disease and infestation. Throughout history it has been used not only to mask unpleasant odours, but also to delight the sense or smell. Like music, colour and taste, a pleasant scent heightens the feeling of wellbeing and is essential for the ambiance of the civilised man. Who cannot remember the aromatic smell of fir needles singed by the lighted candles on the Christmas tree? Is it not recorded that in the genteel homes of the Viennese bourgeoisie sandalwood fuelled the fire used to make the coffee, and that not only in the late Middle Ages, but almost down to the present time, aromatic substances were added to the stove or open fire? Even the most obnoxious pipe tobacco was, and still is, improved with an admixture of lavender. After the tragic death in his sixteenth year of the most intelligent and cultured youth to sit upon a royal throne, Edward VI (1537–1553), a pathetic collection of objects was found in his study, and along with a silver inkpot, sandbox and several astronomical instruments there was a perfume burner and a perfume recipe in his own hand.

As the 16th century came to an end the more primitive containers for aromatic substances were gradually replaced by a more refined vessel, namely the perfume burner. Hand in hand with this development we see the advent of liquid perfume and toilet water. The age of elegance, the rococo period, sees the perfume burner at its most sophisticated and makers vied with one another to produce the finest specimens in metal, pottery and porcelain. The results equal the potpourri vases and scent bottles in beauty (Ill. 27–39). In upper class 19th century homes the perfume burner was an essential part of the inventory and even in the age of neon lighting it can be found under the prosaic name of smoke dispeller (strictly speaking a device for neutralising tobacco smoke).

From the technical standpoint the Brûle-parfum appears in three types. In the simplest – likewise in the so-called perfume lamps or perfume lights – perfumed oil (usually an essential oil, a resin and ambergris, dissolved in olive oil), is burned via a wick. Only the correct balance of ingredients will avoid the production of too much soot.

Standard mixtures were sold as "eau a brûler" or "eau pour brûler"; Eau de

Portugal, Eau de Cologne and Eau Hongroise were usually the basis for these mixtures.

In the 19th century a flameless method was introduced which derived from Dobereiner's principle. Over the wick there was a spongelike platinum part as catalyst which continued to glow after the orignal flame was extinguished. In this way a constant stream of sootless perfume emerged from the openings in the brûle-parfum as long as there was oil in the base.

The third type consisted of a tripod upon which stood a container with pierced lid in which liquid perfume was evaporated. The source of energy was a spirit flame in the base of the vessel (Ill. 28, 33, 35). One should beware, however, of jumping to the conclusion that similar objects either in museums or the antique trade, especially when the lids are missing, are in fact perfume burners: in England similar equipment was used as for keeping tea warm. The burning of aromatic substances, in fact, never fell from favour, but it was in the 18th century, that period in which the pleasures of the senses were indulged with such abandon, including the pleasure of perfume, that there was a fine distinction between sacred fumes and the wafts of scent improving the domestic ambiance. The use of incense was limited strictly to ecclesiastical purposes. New aromatic mixtures were concocted for profane use and along with them, new vessels for their burning. The best known perfume burners are of Meissen manufacture, initially in Bottger stoneware and later in porcelain in the form of small sitting Buddha figures with grinning faces, known as "pagodas" in the Meissen archives. The scent was emitted from their mouths. They are surely among the most curious creations of the European porcelain industry (Ill. 34).

Far removed from the elegant, exclusive and outré objects described above were the pastille burners in the homes of the less affluent; they were, so to speak, the Brûle-parfum of the average person. They appeared on the market in the form of gaily painted miniature houses, churches, or castles in porcelain or pottery. Their range was infinite. Some were mere toys or ornaments for the mantelpiece, others were money boxes, or, with a candle inside, night lights, but many were air improvers in which a mixture of aromatic substances kneaded into a pastille were burnt. The resulting smoke escaped through the chimney of the "edifice". They usually stand on a base (often hollowed out to contain pastilles); some have a removable roof (Fig. 8), others a detachable rear wall. These romantic little buildings were made at various English factories, chiefly Spode and Derby, and appeared on the market in their thousands; there was hardly a 19th century parlour without one, its sweetish heavy scent wafting among the plush upholstery and hangings. Today they are collectors' items and unusual pieces fetch high prices. The pastille burner in Fig. 8 shows a piece of unusual historic interest and there are only two others of its kind extant.

Were these miniature houses and castles a novelty dreamed up to satisfy

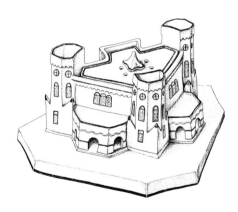

Fig. 8 *Perfume burner representing "Castle House", Aberystwith, Wales built in the Neo-gothic style by John Nash in 1795 for Sir Uvedale Price and demolished in the late 19th century. Sir Uvedale was, like Horace Walpole, an advocate of the gothic revival in England. The roof is removable for the insertion of pastilles. The smoke emerges from the towers which are open at the top. England, Staffordshire, mid 19th century, H. 102 mm. Owned by Mr. Arthur Chater, Richmond, Surrey*

the mass market? On the contrary, they have noble forerunners. Augustus the Strong, King of Saxony, presented the English ambassador, Sir Charles Hanbury, with no fewer than 166 such "buildings", forming an entire village, from his Meissen factory. It is not therefore surprising to read in a Chelsea catalogue of 1756 of a particularly fine perfume container in the form of an old castle. The main "fuels" were scented balls, perfumed candles, aromatic sticks *and material moulded in the shape of animals or leaves*. There are 16th and 17th century references to aromatic creatures known as "Osselets de Chypre". It goes without saying that all materials of this kind, regardless of their form, could be burnt openly and indeed were. There were even trick scented candles with a core of gunpowder.

The recipes for scented candles and pastilles were many and various. Essential to all was a combustible base which did not produce soot, the best being willow charcoal with a binding agent such as Careya Gummi or Gum Arabic (Gummi arabicum, also known as Gum Acacia). To maintain the burning process a little saltpetre or sugar was included, but never both, in order to avoid an explosive mixture. Usually one or more resins (incense, myrrh, storax, maslix, galbanum, benzoin or labdanum), essential as fixatives were added in small quantities to avoid the production of too much smoke. The actual scent came from essential oils (rose oil, patchouli, bergamot oil and oil of sandalwood) sometimes along with small quantities of pulversied aromatic plants such as sandalwood, bay leaves, cinnamon, cloves, rosemary leaves, aniseed, orris, juniper leaves and others. A typical recipe would go as follows:

Willow charcoal (25 parts), finely ground sandalwood (50 parts), bergamot oil (6 parts), lemon oil (4 parts), saltpetre (5 parts), cubeb powder (Piper cubeba) (5 parts), benzoin (25 parts), finely ground cardamon pods (Elettaria cardomomum) (8 parts), myrrh (1–1½ parts), Cascarilla bark (18 parts) and a sufficient quantity of Careya gum. As a fixative musk oil or ambergris (1 part.)

The earliest substances used in western civilisation for the creation of a scented atmosphere were of a solid nature; liquid perfume was unknown before the 17th century. These substances were either completely hardened or ointment-like. An exception was perfumed oil, but it played a relatively minor part, as, for example, in certain religious rites. The perfumes available could not therefore, like our present day ones, be applied to the skin or clothing, so containers had to be made for them from which they would emit a constant even scent. It must also be noted that in the "dark ages" scent was not used for erotic effect but, as was stated in the case of perfume burning, as

Fig. 9 Jörg Ratgeb; portrait of the nobleman Claus Stalburg with rosary and pomander. Germany, 1504. Städelsches Kunstinstitut, Frankfurt

Fig. 10 Apple-shaped needle head. Gold, filled with a resinous paste. Found in the tomb of a prince in Wittislingen (Germany), 6th Ct. BNM

a prophylactic or healing agent. The problem was to invent a container in which these most costly aromatic substances could be carried on one's person which was not hermetically sealed but provided with holes or vents.

There has been much speculation as to why the globe or apple shape was chosen. It probably arises from the original way in which castoreum or castorcum containing substances were prepared: the melted mass was rolled into a ball in the palm of the hand and, when hardened, carried on the person on a string or chain. Evidence of this practice is to be seen from rosaries with beads of aromatic substances dating from the Middle Ages and later. A fine example is to be seen in the Bayerisches Nationalmuseum in Munich. Florentine nobles owned rosaries with beads caged in gold filigree to which was often attached an "oldano" (a large perfumed ball) on a golden chain. In eastern culture the apple was a symbol of eternal life, of the Godhead and of power and strength. We find it on representations of the powerful of this world and in countless paintings and sculptures of the Virgin Mary who holds an apple shaped globe in her hand. A noteworthy example is seen in Francesco Botticini's painting of the Virgin Enthroned (c. 1470) in the Louvre. Paradoxically, in Christian mythology the apple symbolises original sin. On the profane level medicinal powers were long attributed to this fruit: it was said to have a healing effect on the digestive and reproductive systems and to be of help in cases of impotency. It is not certain when the pomander came to Europe from the Arab world where it had been known for a long time. A comprehensive monography reveals that it was first mentioned in literature (as pomme d'ambre) in the middle of the 13th century (Smollich 1983). A century earlier, however, in the year 1174, pomanders were presented to the crusader Emperor Frederick Barbarossa by King Baldwin of Constantinople in gratitude for the former's military assistance against the Infidel. A sixth century ornamental pin in gold from a prince's tomb in Wittislingen, was found to contain aromatic substances in the knob, proof of a much earlier date for this practice. Its oriental origin is indicated in mediaeval descriptions which speak of the "façon de Damaz". In inventories of French treasuries the term "en façon de Grenade" is also used in reference to pomanders.

In England aromatic material was originally sewn into linen bags or carried in silver or gold pierced containers known as "pouncet boxes".

The German for pomander, "Bismapfel", is derived from the word Bisam (musk) and Apfel (apple). It is also referred to as a Bisamknopf (Knopf = knob), particularly when describing smaller ones for attaching to rosaries and, after the 15th century, as decorative items to clothes. The word "Riechapfel" was also used (riechen = to smell) and in French it was variously referred to as a "pomme de musc" or "pomme de senteur", no doubt deriving from the Latin pomum pro odore. Initially musk was the main ingredient of the pomander mixture (see also page 23); not until the 16th century was it rivalled by hardly less costly ambergris. It is this latter substance which gave rise to the name pomander, a contraction of pomme (apple) and ambre (from the French ambre gris or ambre blanc).

A container with a dual function as scent emanator and amulet against all manner of evil has to have apertures. In its simplest form it is a metal sphere which either has holes at top and bottom or all over the surface. There is an example in the Museum of London, the spherical body of which has holes in concentric rows; it is probably early 15th century in date. Unfortunately there are few such early examples. One may assume that since musk was weighed against gold, the wealthy owners who owned pomanders spared no expense and commissioned the best goldsmiths of the day for these items. Even the limited numbers of examples shown here reveal the extent to which these craftsmen were masters of their art, producing pomanders which, either in the simplicity of early specimens or in the intricacy of those of later epochs, are not overshadowed by containers for liquid perfume of later date. All early pomanders have one common characteristic: they are never sub-divided, since they held a single mass of solid aromatic material. They were spherical in form, or almost so, and usually opened into two equal halves by means of a hinge around the "Equator". The two halves were usually held together by a spring release device. At one pole they had a loop and ring and at the other a decorative knob. Only when they were part of a rosary did they have a ring at both poles. The surface between equator and poles showed pierced decoration, from simple gothic tracery, flower heads, fish bladders, and medallions within tracery to fine filigree work with plant motifs (Fig. 43, 46). There are also other combinations where the lower half of the pomander is plain and only the upper half pierced, or one sees examples with a flat base and a slightly pierced area at the upper pole only. Characteristic of the style of pomander prevailing into the 17th century is the omission of a foot or base ring. Some examples are extremely richly ornamented, with the application of diamonds, pearls, garnets, rubies and other precious stones. That is further indication that pomanders were worn by the elite members of society. They were a favoured form of gift from one to another, evidenced by the fact that in 1437 Archduke Siegmund of the Tyrol was the recipient of no fewer than 27 pomanders on one occasion. As well as enabling us to date pomanders, contemporary paintings and prints reveal that they were worn round the neck or suspended from the belt by a chain. Small ones were attached to finger rings by a chain and they were also used as rosary beads. An iconography of the pomander is outside the scope of this book; a few examples only must suffice. There is a typical pomander, worn at the belt, in a painting of the Infanta Maria Anna by Juan Pantoja de la Cruz (1607) in the Kunsthistorisches Museum in Vienna. An early example can be seen in a fresco, "The testament of Moses", by Luca Signorelli (c. 1145–1523) in Orvieto Cathedral in Italy. Another impressive depiction, with all the

Fig. 11 Juan Pantoja de la Cruz; portrait of the Infanta Maria Anna (1606–1646), later wife of Emperor Ferdinand III, at the age of 4–5 months. With the richly embroidered gown as a backdrop the protective ornaments of superstitious belief are evident: relic pendants with Mary monograms, no fewer than nine amulets including a fica, badger's paw, bird's claw, apotropaic bell and pomander. Austria, c. 1607. KHMW

panoply of worldly power, shows one hanging on a golden chain below a medallion studded with jewels in the portrait of a gentleman (c. 1543) by Lucas Cranach. It is in the Württembergische Staatsgalerie in Stuttgart (see also Fig. 9). The inclusion of the pomander on the rosary is splendidly shown in the oak carving of Mary Magdalene dating from c. 1530 in the Archepiscopal Museum in Utrecht. The decline of musk as the main or sole aromatic substance for pomanders, and the necessity of having a number of different ones available at different times and under different circumstances, led to the dividing of the pomander into several sections. Three-compartmented examples, deviating from the classic apple shaped ones but contemporary with them, are common. The subdivision of the spherical pomander brought about the creation of scent containers which are among the most beautiful and complex examples of medieval metalwork. Externally they are of the apple type, although most 16th and 17th century pomanders have a foot or base ring (Ill. 46, 48, 50–53). Whether the subdivision of the pomander was inspired by the segmented structure of oranges and lemons is unsure; purely from the geometrical point of view, the division into vertical segments seemed to be the ideal, and indeed the only possible solution. Although a division into 3 segments of the spherical pomander is conceivable, the lowest number of compartments for this category is four and the largest, eight. The central column, to the base of which the segments are attached with hinges and the angular sides of which correspond to the number of segments, often also has a compartment for yet another aromatic substance. Sometimes, indeed, another compartment, closed or pierced, is built into the foot especially in later examples. This is not infrequently, designed to hold a sponge soaked in liquid scent and is therefore a forerunner of the vinaigrette. When the pomander is closed the segments are secured by a flat to domelike screw lid on which is soldered the loop with carrying ring. Each segment has a perfectly fitting sliding lid with knob or bolt to facilitate opening and is frequently decorated on the sides (Ill. 49). The sliding lids are usually numbered or bear the name of the substance they contain (Ill. 51); occasionally they are embellished with some pattern or other.

Whereas most pomanders are in gold or silver and decorated with embossed or chiselled work, there are enamelled pieces from France and Italy. A particularly splendid example decorated in the Mannerist style came on to the market a few years ago (Launert 1974, Plate 1). In almost all the later pomanders the compartments are completely closed and the scent can only escape when the sliding lid is opened. In 15th century examples, however, the outer wall of each segment is often pierced, as is seen in the specimen in Ill. 49. This piece, which was made by a Rhenish silversmith around 1470, is not only one of the most beautiful of this category of perfume container but is interesting from another point of view. Apart from the open central column containing the figure of a saint, and the reliefs on the sides of the segments

19

recalling the work of the great German sculptors of this period, its outer appearance is also remarkable: the pattern of ribbons with text which ornaments the surface gives the object the appearance of a broken walnut shell making this pomander reminiscent of the Betnüsse (Ill. 63–65) (German beten = to pray, Nuss = nut), a category of amulets. It must be understood at this point that the pomander was not only a container for sweet-smelling substances but also had the function of an amulet; the container itself and its contents were of apotropaic significance. Not infrequently pomanders were worn along with other amulets, indeed, one finds them combined into one object. In the Kriss Collection in the Bayerisches Nationalmuseum there is, to mention but one, a rock crystal amulet joined to a pomander (Fig. 12). In Christian symbolism rock crystal stands for the clarity of the Bible and the purity of Mary. The material and form of an amulet were specific, according to the nature of the evil or illness they were to ward off. Even the precious stones on particularly rich pomanders were not without their apotropaic function. Garnets were said to be effective against the plague and other fever related illnesses. Rubies had a similar intention and were worn to prevent miscarriage. From ancient times the same power was attributed to pearls.

Fig. 12 *Miniature pomander mounted on a flacon-shaped piece of rock crystal. Silver mount. South Germany, 17th/18th Ct. H. 87 mm. BNM*

To understand the significance of the Betnuss one must be familiar with the Doctrine of Signatures which dominated medical practice in the Middle Ages. This associated plants and animals, on the basis of their shape and colour, with similar looking parts and organs of the human body with regard to the healing effect of the former on the latter: the lobe-like leaves of the Hepatica nobilis, a common woodland plant on the continent but absent in the British Isles, were used as a medicament for liver problems because of their resemblance to the shape of the liver; plants with yellow sap were thought to be effective against jaundice; the convoluted surface of the walnut was compared with that of the brain and therefore good for all maladies of a mental nature; for the same reason peach stones and nutmegs were believed to have similar properties. The latter were often crafted in silver and gold and given as love tokens. Nutmeg was also an ingredient of pomander mixtures. This theory is clearly set down in the writings of an English herbalist, William Cole (Adam in Eden, 1657): "... the Kernel hath the very figure of the Brain, and therefore is very profitable for the Brain and resists poysons; For if the Kernel be bruised, and moystned with the quintessence of Wine, and laid upon Crown of the Head, it comforts the Brain and head mightily."

In primitive cultures seeds, especially those with a thickened and textured seed coat, in other words nuts, always had a magical significance. From the seed as from the egg came new life. Seeds, in a seemingly dead condition, survived the onslaughts of the environment, and the prolific offspring of the nut trees symbolised fullness and life force: after all, merely one or two fruits would suffice for the continuation of life. The powers of the germ hidden in the shell were beyond, and still are beyond, the comprehension of mankind. It is not therefore surprising that the adoption of the nut as an amulet, and at the same time as a container for aromatic and magic substances (cf. Ill. 63–65), was by no means coincidental. In the case of the walnut (Juglans regia) there was the additional factor of Christian symbolism, i.e. the cruciform arrangement of the seeds in the opened nut. The mass of superstitious belief that arose with the importation of tropical nuts at the time of the Renaissance is of minor interest to us here (see p. 46 f).

The pomander held sway for several centuries and was not ousted until the 18th century when the smelling box became popular. A series of historically important pieces were the so-called "Royal Portrait Pomanders" which appeared in England in the first quarter of the 17th century and which show a royal portrait on the outer side of each segment (Henry IV, Edward IV, Henry VII, Henry VIII, Elizabeth I). None of these show the same quality of decoration as contemporary continental pieces.

The apple-shaped pomander, as already described, represented the most common form of perfume container and was known throughout western civilisation, but there was also a quantity of different and less complicated types which replaced it or co-existed with it. Of the different forms of cruciform pomander which were first made in the mid-17th century and were a combination of pomander and smelling box only one example can be shown (Ill. 56). In this type of dual purpose object the pomander is small and usually at the upper end. In one example in the Wella Museum in Darmstadt, the lower part is lengthened, an indication that unlike the illustrated piece, it was intended to be held, not worn on a chain. There is a curious specimen in the Science Museum in London (Wellcome Collection) dating from the 17/18th century with seal, pomander, and a whistle along one common axis. Whether the whistle here had the same function as the bell which served to ward off evil, or was to be used in an emergency against footpads is not clear.

As we shall later see in the case of smelling boxes, the heart shape is quite common. This symbolic representation of love – spiritual and carnal – of devotion and friendship needs no explanation. A particularly beautiful example of Frisian workmanship was found in the tomb of Count Anton 1 of Oldenburg (1505–1573) in the church of St. Lambertus in Oldenburg. The back is elegantly pierced but on the front of the silver-gilt capsule we find the signum of Christ above an anchor, and the inscription "in hoc signo vinces". The anchor is the symbol of hope and blessedness. Another deviation from the classic apple shape are egg shaped hanging pomanders with wicker-like openwork, dating from the 18th century; they appear to be limited to Switzerland. More common is the pear shape (Ill. 81), but not until the 18th century. Many examples are notable for their rather overloaded outer decoration of leaves and swags (Ill. 82). Some specimens hardly have the character of a pomander and give rise to doubts whether they should be classified as such or rather as smelling boxes or indeed as vinaigrettes. Among the many other forms of pomander, which really have little to do with its original intention, the snail design is the most frequent (Ill. 66). These imaginative items are not only the offspring of the mediaeval gold and silversmith's competent fantasy, but have a symbolism of their own which can be studied in other branches of the art and folk belief of the time. The ability of the snail to withdraw into its protective shell at times of danger or hardship has resulted in its becoming the symbol of spring and resurrection. We know of the apotropaic use of snail amulets when plague was rife. That the cowrie shell is a symbol of the female sex organ is not surprising. Containers in the form of toads are a rare category (Ill. 57, 58). These creatures, which still inspire an irrational loathing in many people today, were not only the symbol of fertility but also of the dark, lust-driven powers of this world. They were considered to be a protection against the plague and other epidemics. The fish, also a sign of fertility in many cultures, but in ours the symbol of Christian faith, is often found as an amulet, rarely as a pomander, and frequently as a smelling box. One of the curiosities of the treasury of the Munich Residenz is a container in the shape of a bear. When its head is removed a perfume holder is found in the neck. Another bear is in the Kunsthistorisches Museum in Vienna. It is in gold studded with diamonds, rubies and pearls and coated with musk.

Finally, mention must be made of pomanders which are unsurpassed in their morbidity (Ill. 59–62). Skull pomanders were widely found in the lands north of the Alps during the 15th and far into the 16th century. They were mainly of German origin. The open eye-sockets and/or mouth show them to have been pomanders and not smelling boxes. Among several examples of skulls in the British Museum there is a six compartmented one, combined with a lamp. The most interesting is in a private collection in Edinburgh. It is a realistic representation in silver crowned by a laurel wreath. It is housed in a silver container in the form of an apple with stalk and leaves; on one side the imprint of three bites can be seen and on the other the inscription: "A. A. 1628 From Man/Came Woman/From Woman/Came Sin/From Sin Came Death"; apart from the obvious biblical interpretation of these words there are other possible inferences. Very probably the skull and its casing are a remembrance of a victim of syphilis, incurable at the time. As well as simple skulls there are also double faced ones, an allegory of change and decay (Ill. 60–62). Whether the combination of watch and pomander (Ill. 54, 55) is intended as the symbol of the passage of time – tempus fugit – or is merely a superficial conceit is difficult to decide; at all events it is a curious example in the history of scent containers. This may also be said of the apple-like object in illustration 68. On a shell-like silver gilt dish sits the figure of a woman, evidently a rich burgher's wife. She is made in silver and wears a skirt woven out of red material which puffs and bulges out, edged with yellow fringes above and below. This is nothing less than a bag to contain aromatic substances and it is an interesting hybrid between the pomander and the scented cushion discussed elsewhere.

All the objects mentioned in this chapter, with the exception of the latter, are of metal. The combination of a metal pomander with a glass smelling bottle, even in miniature form, is very rare (Ill. 291).

The contents of pomanders

Pomanders, as already indicated, were not only practical and artistically designed containers for solid aromatic substances: their form was also to a large extent of apotropaic significance and that is equally true of the substances they contained. Certainly one of their functions was to mask unpleasant smells, but when one considers that the early contents of the pomander were in themselves evil smelling, it is clear that they had a medicinal function too, and were of a prophylactic and therapeutic nature.

In many cases it was not absolutely necessary to use a medicinal plant in the way would expect it to be used today: alone its presence, and its alleged magic powers would be enough to protect and heal. It was more a lucky charm than a medicine. Merely carrying the plant around with one was thought to ward the plague and other infections, strokes and epilepsy, and to relieve colic and menstrual pain. If a purgative effect was required, the pomander was stuffed with all kinds of not necessarily sweet smelling laxative plants and the desired result was to be obtained by sniffing and inhaling. Since there were all sorts of infections and diseases against which one had to be protected simultaneously, there was a corresponding number of aromatic substances to be carried around, hence the compartmented pomander and the practice of carrying several around at the same time, usually along with amulets of all kind; one took out a comprehensive insurance so to speak. Only by bearing this in mind, can one understand the painting of the Infanta Maria Anna by Juan de la Cruz (1607) in which we note a pomander on the child's belt, a Marian monogram, a fica, a badger's paw, a horn and an apotropaic bell (Fig. 11). To undertake an inventory of all the substances used to fill pomanders mentioned in literature would be very time consuming. In her comprehensive study of the subject (1983) R. Smollich identified 90 substances in 125 recipes and that is not exhaustive. Her compilation of recipes and her studies of plague literature in connection with the theme of pomanders make very worthwhile reading.

Setting aside the use of pure musk in the early days of the pomanders's development, its contents were mainly aromatic resins such as labdanum, benzoin, and storax and plant material such as cinnamon, cloves, iris root, nard (valerian or spike) and Lignum Aloes. To prepare the pomander mixture, several of these ingredients, beginning with the resins, would be

Fig. 13   Small pendant in the form of a book, filled with magic aromatic herbs and/or devotional relics. Found in a woman's grave near Szentes-Nagyhegy, Hungary, late 6th Ct. H. 56 mm. BNM

melted to a syrupy consistency in a pan and then have musk, civet or ambergris added to them in this state. As we know today, these animal secretions were mainly used to stabilise the aromatic mixture. While the mass was still in a pliable state it was rolled into balls in the palm of the hand or pressed into pomander moulds. Space does not permit the analysis of the many recipes. Rosary beads were probably made in the same manner; the beads would be pierced with a needle whilst still warm to provide the necessary threading hole.

Not all pomanders had the most expensive fillings. The less affluent had to make do with more modest and often less agreeable ingredients, for example finely sieved earth mixed with scented substances, and held together with gum or other plant secretions. Even cow dung mixed with beeswax is mentioned.

Additives for therapeutic means include coriander, myrtle oil, the milky juice of spurge (Euphorbia) and even poisonous plants such as henbane (Hyoscyamus niger), the dreaded hemlock (Conium maculatum) and opium poppy (Papaver somniferum).

The use of pomanders in general, and their contents in particular, was by no means universally acclaimed. At various times enlightened doctors and priests attacked what they saw as superstitious belief. In his "Anatomy of Abuses" of 1583 Philip Stubber, a puritan, spoke out clearly against the folly of the pomander cult: "These intrusive aromas, smoke clouds, vapours and scents of musk, civet, pomanders, perfumes, balsams and such, reaching the brain, abase, dull and stunt the spirit and the senses, instead of in some way sharpening and enlivening them."

The satirical work "Stulte olfactionis scapha" (The Boat of Foolish Odours) of 1502 by the German Jodocus Badius is to be interpreted as declaration of war more against worldly vanity than against spurious medicinal benefit, since in the caricature of similar title, "Das Boot der törichten Frauen" (The Boat of Foolish Women), a street vendor is in the act of offering pomanders for sale to the occupants of the small ship.

In the applied arts one constantly runs into difficulty in the classification of artefacts because the lines of demarcation are both temporal and material. In the case of perfume holders, form and construction are not only determined by the contents but also dependent on the way in which the contents are to be used. Soldid and liquid perfumes require to be kept and used differently.

Let us remain, briefly, with the pomander, which had two functions as a container – the holding of solid aromatic substances and the diffusion of the scents that emanated from them. For the first function a container which could be closed was needed, for the second a pierced surface. As has been said in the preceding chapter, a series of containers, linked in such a way that the whole may still be classified as a pomander, fulfilled both requirements. The segmented pomander, with individual compartments closed by means of sliding or lifting lids, was in practice a smelling box with several compartments, the contents of which could be enjoyed singly or in combination. What all these containers, open or closed, had in common, was in fact the nature of their contents, namely solid perfume, and solid perfume remained in favour a long time after the liquid form came into use. What in the course of time, more exactly in the 17th century, went out of fashion was the pomander itself.

The smelling box is the link between the pomander and scent bottle, until the latter began virtually to lead the field in the 18th century. For the pedantic the term box in connection with perfumes is perhaps far too vague. It is true that it appeared in every possible and indeed every impossible form. In England there were walking sticks carried by plague doctors on visits to their patients, with smelling boxes built into the ivory handle (Fig. 14). Sir Charles Jackson mentions such a stick in the year 1613, and another is alleged to have belonged to Charles I and to have been used by him during his captivity on the Isle of Wight in 1647.

Apart from these two examples, smelling boxes are usually exclusively made of metal, generally silver and gold. They were not uncommonly made in the form of books. The oldest piece of this kind is in the Kriss Collection in Munich and comes from the tomb of a woman in Eastern Hungary and is dated 6th century (Fig. 13). In the Science Museum in London (Wellcome Collection) there is an English example from the early 17th century with three compartments for aromatic substances. A particularly fine example is in the British Museum (illustrated in H. Taite, 1963): The "book" is c. 50 mm high, has a pierced lid with mannerist decoration, is black and white enamelled and ornamented on each corner with a shallow cut diamond; it opens by means of a sliding lid underneath.

It is no surprise to find the heart motif in smelling box designs. Here smelling box and amulet overlap. As a symbol of divine love (Heart of Jesus and Heart of Mary representations show this clearly) the heart is a most important symbol in religious folk belief, hence the great quantity of heart shaped smelling boxes. If two billing doves sit on the heart, we have a reference to earthly love (Ill. 92, 93). From the Alpine regions there are smelling boxes dating from the 17/18th century which have a rock crystal mounted on the heart (Fig. 12).

Finally the animal world is a rich source when we are considering the form of smelling boxes. We find mainly fish (Ill. 98, 100–102) and snails (Ill. 97). Snail containers with pierced walls are not uncommon, qualifying in fact as pomanders; they were often worn as plague amulets. In the Museum für

Fig. 14 Walking stick for a doctor for use when visiting plague victims or patients in malodorous or infectious situations. The knob, in silver piqué work, has a lid which is perforated and unscrews to reveal a compartment for aromatic substances or a sponge soaked with vinegar. England, 1st h. 18th Ct. P. England

Kunst und Gewerbe in Hamburg among other smelling boxes in animal form we can see a sitting lion, heraldic in spirit (Ill. 99). Some of the most extravagant examples of animal inspired smelling boxes are in the form of man's best friend. Still within the animal kingdom we have the egg (Ill. 69, 76–79). In a category of their own are boxes which were made in Denmark in the 18th and early 19th century, principally in Copenhagen and the small town of Tondern. They are unsurpassed in their variety by any other form of smelling box. A typical one consists of an urn-shaped silver container standing upright on a base or foot, its decoration ranging from the rocaille of the late rococo to the classical forms of the second half of the 19th century. They are often studded with overdimensional "gems" in garishly coloured glass. Some of these extravagant artefacts, which from their appearance must have been bridal gifts, are attributed to well known silversmiths such as Peter Johann Petersen and were made between 1830 and 1835. The Municipal Museum in Altona, near Hamburg has an entire showcase full of these peculiar objects. Traces of material inside them and others of the same period reveal that they contained, not solid perfume, but a scent soaked sponge, showing them to be the forerunner of the vinaigrette. In some there is a special compartment in the base for a miniature scented cushion (Ill. 92–95, 103–107).

The Vinaigrette

The increasing use of liquid perfume in the course of the 18th century demanded a new type of container. The practice of resorting to aromatic substances as a preventative measure against infectious diseases was practically forgotten; a routine of personal hygiene that left much to be desired, heavy hairstyles, elaborate clothing and, above all, poorly ventilated houses, even though they might be palaces, and a strictly regulated manner of living, where the faint had its place in the code of manners, clearly demanded perfumes to revitalise and revive (Fig. 15).

Among the substances which, before the introduction of ammonia in the 19th century, were most effective in stimulating the mucous membranes of the nose, thereby leading to an increase in the supply of blood to the brain, was vinegar, or more correctly acetic acid, hence the arrival on the scene in the last years of the 18th century of the "vinaigres parfumés", that is liquid scents. Boxes were obviously unsuitable for liquids, certainly if the liquids were of a corrosive nature, in which case incidentally they would also be irritant, if not downright dangerous, to skin or eyes. Since the liquids were volatile and were not needed for more than a few seconds at a time (whoever doubts this should try breathing in a perfume of that period for a longer time), a hermetically sealable and spill-free container was essential. In England this resulted in the vinaigrette, which, no matter how varied the

Fig. 15 *French caricature of J. Platier (active c. 1840) demonstrating the use of Pomade (grease based aromatic substances) "Lion pomade is no less than the fat of African lions fed on jasmine and aromatic plants. It is an excellent remedy for hair loss, destroys fleas, improves the breath and cures sight defects, skin eruptions, epilepsy, physical and political ills. It has helped kings, princes, generals and even police presidents". C. Schwarzkopf*

ions d'Afrique nourris au jasmin et aux plantes
,la destruction des punaises , la purification de
, épileptiques, organiques et politiques .Elle a
res de police. Le 'Constitutionnel , le Gratis , et

outward form, followed a basic pattern. The container is provided with a well fitting lid and inside, under a removable grille, is a sponge soaked in the desired scent (Ill. 110).

A forerunner of the vinaigrette was the smelling box with pierced lid known from the time of Elizabeth I onwards. It was known variously as a „pouncet box" (after the late 16th and early 17th century) and a "sponge box" (after the mid 17th century). In most vinaigrettes the inside is lined with gold to avoid corrosion and undesirable smell caused by chemical reaction between metal and content.

The vinaigrette was as short lived as the social environment which had made it necessary. Invented in the latter years of the 18th century, it reached its height of popularity and widest use – as can be ascertained from the hall marks – between 1820 and 1850, and it very quickly disappeared in the third quarter of the 19th century, when it was replaced by the less cumbersome and cheaper smelling bottles.

Although the structure of vinaigrettes was simplicity itself, they lent themselves to a wealth of imaginative design as far as outward appearance was concerned. Many are minor masterpieces of the English gold and silversmiths; others on the other hand are the height of vulgarity. The nature of the grille in itself is noteworthy: early examples show simple geometrical piercings or stylised patterns; these are followed by harmonious lace-like designs, which when the vinaigrette was at its zenith, become the wildest arabesques. In vinaigrettes of the usual box form the lid is the vehicle for design. It can consist of a large semi-precious stone, but it is usually silver and either engraved or repoussé. Cast lids also occur. The motifs are as varied as on tabatières, snuff boxes or other silver items of the same period, but predominate on vinaigrettes townscapes and architectural themes, especially cathedrals and royal residences. It would be possible to start a topographical collection based solely on these. The description of all the types of vinaigrette would be a book in itself: no theme or motif is missing. The imitation book in all sizes and "bindings" was popular, then of course here again we have the heart and that other pledge of love, the padlock, often combined with each other. The question remains open as to how one can equate the sharp irritations of the olfactory nerves with love. And so it goes on, unlimited: acorn, chrysanthemum, rose, thistle, poppyseed case, strawberries, various types of wreaths, shells, snails, birds, fish, cows, guns, cornucopias, tortoises, lanterns, bellows, champagne bottles, and, hard to believe, indelicate if not obscene objects which defy description and even today would not be shown in museum cases.

The frequency of topographical associations leads us to speculate about the development of the early souvenir industry and it could be linked to the growth of the railway network. In all these vinaigrettes with views it is noticeable that the motif, be it a castle, cathedral or country scene, fills the entire lid surface. This perhaps gives a laboured and less than elegant effect but has a practical purpose; metal pressed or hammered into relief is more stable than a smooth surface, and one could also economise on the quantity of silver used to make the vinaigrette lid.

Vinaigrettes of non-metallic materials, such as ivory, glass and wood belong to the later period of this kind of container and overlap with smelling bottles, with which they finally appear in combination (Ill. 299, 319, 345–348). All vinaigrettes, independent of form and workmanship, have characteristics in common: they were small and often delicate. The concentrated nature of their contents made a larger vessel unecessary, and they belonged to that collection of objects carried on the person, so had to fit easily into a gentleman's pocket or a lady's bag or muff. They could also be worn as jewellery, on a chain.

The centre of vinaigrette manufacture as hallmarks witness was Birmingham, followed by London. According to Delieb (1970) there are only two Dublin examples and the genre was unknown on the Continent. The most important makers were Nathaniel Mills and Matthew Linwood of Birmingham and, as far as manufacturers of the later period were concerned, the firm of S. Mordan & Co., which will be mentioned frequently in this book, played a great part.

So much for the containers, but what did they contain? The vital element was acetic acid, its pungent, irritating effect on the mucus membranes of the nostrils made more agreeable by aromatic substances, if not eliminated entirely. The most famous solution for daily use consisted of concentrated acetic acid (28 grams) and rose oil (1.75 grams); more rarely eau de cologne was chosen. The scent character was obtained from the oils of rosemary, lavender, angelica root, clove and camphor. Tested recently by the author, this mixture gave a pungent sensation fading into a pleasant scent after a while, and it was found to be effective against headaches and lassitude. There are dozens of recipes involving the use of marjoram, sweet flag (*Acorus*), cinnamon, wormwood (*Artemisia*), Roman wormwood (*Artemisia pontica*), peppermint, rue (*Ruta graveolens*), coriander, nutmeg and even garlic. Finally, one of the curiosities in perfume history is a legendary mixture, said to have had prophylactic powers, which went under the name of "Vinaigre des Quatre Voleurs", or in pharmacists' language, acetum quattuor latronum. This witches' brew consisted of acetic acid, brandy, Roman mugwort, rosemary, sage, peppermint, rue, lavender, cinnamon, sweet flag, nutmeg and garlic. Its history is worth recounting: during an outbreak of plague in Marseilles four rogues were arrested who had claimed to be male nurses but who did nothing but steal the wordly goods of the poor victims of the disease. They themselves seemed to be immune from the plague, because they carried a magic potion around with them. Their revelation of the recipe saved their skin.

Fig. 16 Representation of an elegant lady sampling her perfume recipe. Note the bottle she holds in her hand, and the trough containing a specimen of Rosa centifolia *near the table set up in the open air. Hand coloured print on the lid of a box of mixed perfumes. France, said to be 18th Ct. but most probably later. Parfumerie Fragonard, Grasse*

To round off this account of the vinaigrette, mention must be made of a scent container which preceded it and which was relatively short-lived, namely the essence box. It usually had a sliding lid and occasionally had a hinge. Under the grill instead of a sponge there was a mixture consisting of rice starch, magnesium carbonate and pounded iris root. It is evident that the more effective vinaigrette would soon have ousted such a basic predecessor.

SMELLING BOTTLES

The collector of small glass items will not always find it easy to recognise smelling bottles as such. Medicine bottles are generally recognisable through their simplicity and lack of ornament; they serve a practical purpose and were seldom reused. The case of snuff containers is different. Apart from the wealth of snuff boxes, the late 18th and particularly the 19th century saw the adoption in increasing numbers of the snuff bottle. They were made in stoneware, porcelain and above all in glass. These bottles were made of blown glass in the glass houses of the Fichtelgebirge (Germany) and the Bohemian Forest and neighbouring areas well known for their forests. In form and variety they are not so different from the perfume bottles made in the same regions. They differ, however, in size, in having a wider neck, and in the type of stopper, either in wood or metal. Only better examples possess their own cut glass stoppers and these are the ones which could be falsely identified as smelling bottles.

"Nachbarin, Euer Fläschchen" (Madame Neighbour, your phial), a quotation from Goethe's Faust, often used, ridiculed and misunderstood, could serve as a heading for this chapter (Fig. 16). Directly related to the vinaigrette, historically preceding it, coexisting with it and outlasting it, it is one of those scent containers whose contents served a secondary purpose, that of a therapeutic and prophylactic nature. It was perhaps initially filled with the same mixtures as the vinaigrette, but in the coarse of the 19th century, preparations were increasingly introduced which had a more rapid and dramatic effect on the mucus membranes of the nose.

The bottles were filled with liquid ammonia on its own or mineral salts containing pungent substances such as ammonia, carbolic acid, eucalyptus oil, menthol and others. To moderate or render more pleasant the sharp prickly effect of ammonia, perfumes were added to the mixture, principally lavender.

Smelling salts were sold under various names such as "inexhaustible salt", "Eau de Luce", and "Sal volatil" and French recipe books speak of "Sel anglais à base d'ammoniaque". A typical composition was: liquid ammonia (0.56 l), lavender essence (1.77 g), bergamot essence (0.88 g), rosemary essence (1.77 g), and cloves (0.88 g). Most popular at the waning of the 19th century was the so-called white smelling salt, also known as Preston salt (Sel de Preston). They were slower to fade than the other recipes, the result of the addition of sesqui-carbonate of ammonia. In less well known recipes the addition of musk and ambergris was required. The great difficulty of developing a container suitable for these mixtures arose from their corrosive effect, their tendancy to evaporate, and the problem of spillage. With the exception of gold and silver metal was, as for the vinaigrettes, unsuitable. Porcelain and glazed stoneware were used (Ill. 188, 189), but glass was by far the most common material. A milky clouded inner surface indicates that a bottle was used for smelling salts. Since the evaporation rate of ammonia and other solvents is linked to temperature, most of the hand held bottles were not only made of thick glass, but also deeply cut to lower the level of heat conduction. The cut surfaces with their high light reflection and/or the use of coloured or flashed glass served to hide either the liquid inside the bottle or its corrosive effect of the interior surface.

As vehicles for the scent a sponge was used in the early days, following the practice for vinaigrettes, which largely reduced the attractiveness of a clear glass bottle. In the second half of the century it was replaced by coarse crystals of sulphur carbonate. To avoid spillage during use the bottle neck was stopped with cotton wool. Bottles in this condition are still to be found in drawers or old handbags: the pungent ammonia has, it is true, evaporated but the perfume additive is still discernible after a century.

Since premature evaporation and the oxidisation of the contents was to be avoided, particular attention had to be paid to the method of closure. Cork stoppers were unattractive and unreliable; ground glass stoppers usually sealed effectively but were expelled by gas pressure if the contents warmed up, ruining many a handbag or coat pocket. If unused for a long time as many collectors of these small bottles know to their cost, it could also happen, that the stopper became lodged in the neck through corrosion.

Victorian ingenuity solved the problem, in the form of the spring-hinged lid which in the latter years of the 19th century, swept across the world from its centres of origin, Birmingham and London. Behind a rim in the metal cap there is a glass disc which is pressed against the plain ground top surface of the bottle by a strong metal spring, thus sealing the bottle hermetically. Slight pressure applied to the release button (Ill. 348) is sufficient to make the cap spring open. The reliability of this device can still be demonstrated on old bottles. The main manufacture was the firm of S. Mordan. Other closures, such as the one patented by the firm of Cooper, in which a glass marble is pressed against the opening of the neck by a cap, were less effective and are consequently less frequently found.

When we study the larger collections in museums or specialised antique shops, or look through contemporary catalogues, it becomes clear just how popular smelling bottles were in the second half of the 19th century. The main centres of manufacture were London and Birmingham, where, among many, particular mention must be made of the firms of S. Mordan, Howel & Co., Maw and Son, Howel James & Co., and Thompson. One of the most important stockists was R. H. Barrett in The Oval in Hackney (London). Whether he also made smelling bottles is not certain. His advertisements offer all sorts of bottles and especially those with metal caps and reliable closure. Whoever still has recourse to smelling salts today must buy a rather unattractive disposable brown glass bottle from the chemist's. The time when the smelling bottle was a fashionable accessory is long past.

SCENTED CUSHIONS AND POT-POURRIS

The flower is as ephemeral as its scent, and scented flowers are not obtainable during every season or in every place. For centuries, long before the introduction of liquid perfume, people have made scented cushions, stuffing them with dried flower heads and other plant parts. Pliny mentions the use of dried mixed blossoms to perfume rooms. Apart from the strewing of dried flowers in living quarters, churches, hospitals and other public buildings, two other ways of using them have developed in Europe since the Middle Ages, namely the scented cushion and the pot-pourri. Whereas the latter is intended to perfume a room, the scented cushion, or sachet, has several functions. The herb mixtures sewn into silk, linen, or other material served not only to perfume linen in cupboards but to keep moths and other pests away. In addition the scented cushion was used in therapy: filled with the required medicinal plants (valerian or camomile flowers, for example) and laid under the pillow at night, it was said to help insomnia and other nervous afflictions. The composition of the stuffing is not essentially different from the pot-pourri mixture, except that the materials are pounded or at least roughly chopped. In many cases a single plant species is used, usually lavender; from the Biedermeier period cushions stuffed with mignonette (*Reseda*) are known.

When preparing a pot-pourri mixture one should bear in mind that most flowers are scentless in their dried state. Exceptions are lavender, marjoram, thyme and rosemary. Even rose petals, the basis of most mixtures, lose their delicate scent completely unless they are gathered early in the morning on a dry day from flowers which have just opened. They must then be left to dry, in a warm airy place, but never in the sun, and on no account should, they be tightly packed. Certain recipes require rosebuds which, freshly picked, are to be dried in dry sand in a stoneware pot in a warm place. Instead of sand, coarse sugar is also recommended. Plants with aromatic leaves and flowers that are not easily detached were strewn loose, or in bunches, between the layers of linen in the cupboard. Particularly charming are the "Lavender

Dollies" made in England and also in Portugal. There are certain plants which have a stronger scent in the dried condition than in the fresh (sweet woodruff, for example), and certain leaves or barks only develop one as they dry.

The word pot-pourri appeared in the 18th century. It is derived from the French pourrier = to rot (Latin putrere). In Spanish is is known as Olla podrida. Unknown in England until 1749, it is first mentioned in a letter of that year written by a Lady Luxborough, ... "which is a potful of all kinds of flowers which are several perfumes, and commonly when mixed and rotten, smell very ill". The original mixture consisted of rose and orange flowers with small quantities of other herbs and spices. Later, with new exotic plants arriving in Europe, the recipes became increasingly richer and more complicated.

There is a distinction between dry and moist pot-pourris. As the name indicates, all the contents of a dry pot-pourri are in a dried condition. A traditional pot-pourri contains approximately 1 Litre (volume) of rosepetals, 50 g Lavender flowers, 30 g sweet woodruff, 30 g common melilot, 30 g rosemary, 5 g thyme, 50 g orris powder, 7 g grated nutmeg, 7 g cloves, 7 g cinnamon, 7 g mace and 12.15 g benzoin.

For a moist pot-pourri the basis is half dried flowers (usually roses), laid between layers of salt in a stoneware jar which is then closed and left to stand in a warm place for three months. The resulting damp mass is then mixed with other dry ingredients such as lavender, orris powder, vanilla, thyme, cassia, cloves, sweet woodruff, benzoin, cubeb and sweet flag.

The known number of recipes would fill a book. Almost every noble house in England had its own mixture; the most luxurious ones contained sugar, very costly at the time, and brandy. To lengthen the mixture's life – a good one should last a year – the addition of an odourless fixative (see also page 35 f) is necessary. As well as the benzoin and orris powder one finds admixtures of sweet flag, ambergris, storax, balsam of Peru, patchouli oil and others.

If a pot-pourri is to be effective, it must be placed centrally in the room and be large enough to allow for an adequate diffusing surface. In this way it becomes quite an important element in the room's furnishings. It has the same role as a flower vase. In its simplest form it is a flat decorative porcelain or stoneware bowl. In England's earlier colonial days flower decorated porcelain dishes from the Far East were favoured. They are still to be found in some mansions. To improve its appearance non-scented but colourful flowers were added to the mixture. However attractive and popular, and however widespread such bowls were, they were nevertheless real dust collectors. No wonder, therefore, that in the late 17th century pot-pourri vases were introduced. These could be closed yet allow the scent to escape through a perforated lid and not unusually a pierced body. There is hardly a

European porcelain manufacture which is not represented by them, and particular mention must be made of Sevres, Meissen and Nymphenburg. In form and decoration these showpieces reflect the style of their period, from Mannerism to the powerful lines of the Baroque, to the delightful exuberances of the Rococo and to the sober self-conscious creations of Neo-classicism, and they vie with other table ornaments of their day, with the splendid vases, soup tureens, dinner services, perfume burners and other decorative objects, as fruits of a highly developed civilisation (Ill. 39–42).

The Greeks are said to have been the first people to use liquid perfume, not perfume as we understand it, but finely ground aromatic substances of plant origin suspended in oil. Women were mainly responsible for its preparation, but it was Theophrastus of Eresos who, in 4 B. C., first wrote about the art of perfumery and pointed out the detrimental effect of light on scented substances.

Real perfume was only made possible by the advent of distillation. It is supposed that there had been primitive distillation equipment in Ancient Egypt, but it was the Arabs who mastered the process and by the 9th–10th century were able to isolate an essential oil (from juniper wood). Around the year 900 Avicenna, the greatest scientist in the Arab world, succeeded in extracting essential oil from flowers, especially those of the rose.

Through the Arabs this epoch-making discovery came to medieval Europe. Only now could the traditional scented materials for burning and solid perfume substances be replaced by liquids. Thanks to the process of distillation the list of suitable plant materials could be extended in a way undreamed of hitherto and each one could be exploited in larger quantities. In European monasteries, and through the medical practices of the West, the method was constantly being improved. Lavender water first appeared in 1150, its discovery attributed to Saint Hildegard of Bingen, and possibly the first perfume namely Eau de Hongrie was created around 1370. According to legend it was made up by a hermit for the ageing but still beautiful Queen Elizabeth of Hungary.

The earliest scientific work on distillation is the *Destillierbuch* (1500), illustrated with very expressive woodcuts by Hieronymus Braunschweig, a Strasburg physician. This was followed by a further handbook on the method, which concerns itself principally with eau de toilette, namely the *Coelum Philosophicum* (1526) of Phillipp Ulstadt of Nuremberg. In 1556 another step forward came with a comprehensive work by another Strasburg doctor, Walter Hermann Ryff, *Das New Gross Destillierbuch*, in which the production of countless essential oils is described for the first time. *Les Secrets de Maistre Alexys le Piedmontois* (1555), whose real name was Girolamo Ruscelli, is the first book in French literature on perfume. In this work there is a recipe which is said to guarantee a woman lasting beauty: "Take a young raven from its nest, feed it for forty days on hard boiled eggs; kill and distil it with myrtle leaves, almond oil and talc." The foundation stone of the French perfume industry had been laid, it is true, a long time previously by the issuing of a patent by Henry VI in 1426 in connection with the manufacture of scented gloves, but it was not until the end of the 17th century that France outdid Italy in the art of perfumery, although the latter country had had a laboratory for perfume manufacture in operation in the convent of Santa Maria Novella in Florence since 1508. The basic materials for perfume, with the exception of modern synthetic products come, mainly

Fig. 17 Panel of tiles: "The Sense of Smell". Painted in monochrome by Jan Almis. Netherlands, Rotterdam, 1764. MKG

Fig. 18 Shop sign for a soap and perfume shop in the City of London (now placed outside a bank in Kensington High Street, London).

from the plant kingdom and to a small extent from the animal world. Plants supply aromatic resins, balsams and essential oils. Out of a quarter of a million flowering plants, less than 2000 possess these readily evaporable ingredients, and out of this second figure only relatively few are suitable for perfumery.

Only in a few cases it the entire plant of use (mint, rosemary, sage, lavender, lippia and a few others). The following plant parts are used: the flower (rose, jasmine, mimosa, carnation, narcissus, acacia, tuberose, orange and – hardly ever today – violet), leaves (pelargonium, orange, laurel, bergamot, patchouli), fruit or seed (vanilla, caraway, aniseed, musk-seed, clove, nutmeg etc.), fruit peel (orange, bergamot, lemon), wood (sandalwood, camphor tree, pine, cedar, rosewood), bark (cinnamon, cascarilla (*Croton elutheria*), root (ginger, iris, sassafras, vetiver, angelica). Even a lichen, *Evernia prunastri* is used, mainly as a fixative. The resins and balsams include labdanum, styrax and benzoin. Oranges are used in three ways: the petals give the pure and costly "orange flower absolute" and the less expensive neroli oil, the leaves and twigs the so-called "petit grain", and the peel contains the actual orange oil.

It is not within the scope of this book to give a detailed account of the various ancient and modern extraction and distillation processes and the complicated methods of composition in perfume making.

Only in a few cases does the essential oil mirror the scent of the plant from which it was obtained. Most perfumes bearing a floral name have, in fact, been created from other basic materials by the perfumer in the laboratory. Indeed, perfumes have been marketed which bear the names of scentless plants or those which cannot yield their scent, such as cyclamen, fougère (fern) or lily of the valley, and which are derived from other substances, both natural and synthetic.

Three phases of fragrance are recognised when considering almost all the essential oils and the perfumes of which they form part. The perfumer refers to them as "notes". These are the "note de tête" (top note), "note de coeur" (middle note) and the "note de fond" (end note). The "note de tête" is very volatile and is sensed as soon as the bottle is opened. For this reason a perfume must not be chosen on the basis of a whiff from a bottle. The "note de coeur" is the real character of the perfume and reveals itself only when the perfume is in contact with the skin and when the "note de tête" has completely disappeared. Finally the "note de fond" reflects the lasting quality of the perfume on warm skin. This and the intensity of the fragrance depends on the perfumer's, choice of fixative, that is, on the substance which brings all the components that go to make a perfume into a state of balance. Here the art of the perfumer is well and truly tested, for almost all fixatives possess a rather strong smell of their own.

Certain of the raw materials already mentioned provided by the animal kingdom, are still essential for the production of fine perfumes. Like oak moss (see above), their main function is to stabilise a perfume and thereby lengthen the period of its effectiveness. They had the same function in the solid perfume mixtures and pot-pourri recipes long before the advent of liquid perfume. Ambergris of legendary fame is now only of historical interest, but a thousand years ago was a source of wealth for Eastern traders. It is produced in the intestines of the sperm whale (Physeter catodon) was used mainly for perfumes with a balsam note and. It is found drifting in soft fatty lumps on the seas. Today it is replaced by synthetic substances. The same goes for civet, a concentrated, penetrating and foul smelling secretion reminiscent of cat excreta, produced by a sex gland in both sexes of the civet cat (Viverra civetta). When greatly diluted, however, it has a pleasant smell. It was particularly favoured for perfumes with an oriental note. Today it too is almost completely replaced by synthetics.

Still greatly in demand is castoreum, obtained from pearshaped glands situated near the genitalia of the beaver (castor fiber) (Fig. 20). In medieval times it was used as an antispasmodic drug. In perfumery it is used as fixative, particularly in perfumes with a leather or tobacco note, therefore mainly for gentlemen's toiletries.

Musk has been of prime importance in the making of all kinds of aromatic preparations for many centuries and it is by far the most long lasting and penetrating of all substances used. Its fragrance can still be detected in Arab mosques built more than a thousand years ago with mortar containing musk. Captains of tea clippers from the Far East would never take musk on board, no matter how well sealed, for fear of spoiling their cargo. Still highly valued by perfumers, it has a pungent faecal smell in concentrated form. It comes from the sex glands of the male musk deer (Moschus moschiferus), which lives unobtrusively at great heights in the mountains of China, Tibet and the Himalayas (Fig. 19). Similar substances, but by no means of equal quality, are obtained from the musk rat (Ondatra zibethicus) and certain exotic reptiles.

The production of synthetic substances began in the year 1833 when Dumas, having experimented with terpenes, found a formula for anethole (a constituent of the oils of fennel and aniseed), borneol (present in the oils of lavender, rosemary and other plants), and camphor. In 1834 Mitscherlich synthesised the first cheap odorant with nitrobenzene. Liebig and Wöhler produced benzaldehyde which reproduced the smell of bitter almond oil and which became very important for the perfume industry. From then onwards hardly a year passed in which new aromatic substances were not created in the retort. It is a gallery of famous names in the annals of science: Calhours, Perkin, Reimer, Tiemann, Herzfeld, Tilden, Wallach, Baur and so on, up to 1920 when Ruzicka examined the chemical structure of musk and in 1933

Fig. 19 Musk deer (Moschus moschiferus), a rare and timid animal mostly confined to mountain regions of China, the Northern Himalayas and Tibet. Abdominal glands near its genital organs contain musk. This substance can also be found in the musk-ox (Ovibos moschatus) and in the musk-rat (Ondatra zibethicus).

Fig. 20 Beaver (Castor fiber), a rodent of aquatic habitats with a flat short tail and webbed hind legs. In pear-shaped glands situated near the genitalia the Castoreum is produced. The yellowish-brown castoreum from Siberian animals is supposed to be superior in quality to the reddish black substance yielded by Canadian beavers.

36

discovered the formula for jasmone which is a constituent of jasmine. In the fifties modern methods such as gas chromatography, ultraviolett spectroscopy, rotation dispersion and other processes rationalised the witches' cauldrons of the past.

Synthetic perfumes can be divided into two groups: those imitating a natural scent and those which introduce totally new scents unknown in nature. They have by no means ousted all natural materials: every first-class perfume still contains a proportion of plant extracts. The exception is the violet, the fragrance of which for economic reasons is nowadays always of synthetic origin.

Synthetic ingredients must by no means be regarded as inferior materials; in some cases they are dearer than the natural products. Their advantage, and this they have in common with synthetic medicines, is that they are independent of weather and soil conditions and they are always available in the same consistent quantities. In addition they have given modern perfumers a scope unknown to their famous counterparts of the past such as René, Houbigant (Fig. 21), Pivet, Millot, Lilly, Rimmel and Chardin, to name only the most celebrated. In Eugene Rimmel's day the perfumer had at his disposal about 500 aromatic substances; today the palette for his compositions comprises thousands.

Our subject is essentially that of scent bottles. To understand their use, however, it is necessary to know something about perfume categories for they, for one thing, determine the size of the bottle.

Fig. 22   "Rosolenflasche". The earliest commercial scent bottle for Eau de Cologne. Dark green Waldglas. In the background an advertising sheet pointing out the medical value of the preparation. (Eau de Cologne has been sold merely as a toilet preparation only since 1810.) Germany, 17th Ct. Messrs. Farina Gegenüber, Cologne

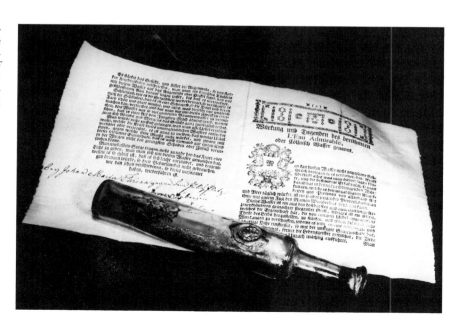

Pure perfume, also known as an "extrait", consists 12–20% of essences of various scented substances; the rest is alcohol, with a modest addition of distilled water. It is always dear and is sold, on account of its limited life when the stopper is frequently removed, in small, efficiently sealable flacons.

If the essence content is a mere 8–10%, we have an "Eau de Senteur" or "Eau de Parfum". Its scent is not so heavy as in the case of pure perfumes, but it is still intensive enough. It is usually sold in larger bottles. Both types are light and heat sensitive and should therefore be stored accordingly.

A classic Eau de toilette or toilet water is generally characterised by a single scented component (rose, lavender or violet water) and contains between 5 and 8% of the corresponding essential oils. It can be more liberally splashed on because of its less intense perfume, after the bath for example or as a hair tonic, and is, therefore, sold in larger bottles (Ill. 263, 264, 288, 338, 372).

Eau de Cologne or Kölnischwasser, as it is known in Germany, is usually lighter than eau de toilette and contains about 2–4% of the essential oils of bergamot, lemon, orange, neroli, lavender and rosemary, according to the brand. It is also retailed in large bottles of a characteristic type for this product (Fig. 22). Its history, dominated by the figure of Johann Maria Farina (1685–1766), is as interesting as it is delightful (Fig. 23). The firm of "Farina Gegenüber" in Cologne closed a few years ago after a tradition of two centuries.

Eau de toilette and Eau de Cologne are both eminently suitable for the perfume spray, which has been around since the latter years of the 19th century, showing many forms and various spraying mechanisms (Ill. 277, 284, 287, 339, 356, 371).

Fig. 23   Johann Maria Farina (1685–1766). Founder of the "Eau de Cologne" industry. Messrs. Farina Gegenüber, Cologne

One of the earliest and finest examples of an anointing oil flacon in metal is one dating from the last quarter of the 13th century in the Königliche Kunstkammer (Royal Treasury) in Berlin (now in the Kunstgewerbemuseum, Inv. Nr. K. 4198). Anointing oils for ritual purposes were rarely perfumed; the church usually used pure olive oil and that is very largely the case today. Containers for it are therefore of no interest to us here. Equally outside the scope of this book are the Far Eastern, particularly Chinese, bottles in precious or semi-precious stone made for fragrances.

In the West, the history of the scent bottle begins in the 16th century with containers in precious metal or semi-precious stone; this category reaches its zenith in the 17th century, but is largely, if not totally, replaced by bottles in less valuable materials in the course of the 18th.

In contrast with bottles in other materials – and this is true also of later periods – almost all bottles in precious metals are unique examples. They

FLACONS IN METAL AND SEMI-PRECIOUS STONE

were commissioned singly by some nobleman or by the monarch, in other words by people of standing and wealth. As the pomander once was, the scent bottle now became an integral part of the toilette or the table and was a status symbol, the reflection of its owner's social standing, often more important in this role than in that of scent container.

The scent bottles of the Renaissance must be considered along with other small and precious artefacts as part and parcel of their owners dress and social position (in museum showcases they are isolated as 'interesting objects', like mummies whose souls fled their bodies thousands of years ago). Yet they were not solely dress and table accessories, but were an essential part of the treasury of every self respecting Renaissance prince. Albrecht V, Duke of Bavaria, was one of the great collectors of precious objects, and the treasures that Emperor Rudolf II amassed for the glory of his court and the House of Hapsburg, including several scent bottles, are almost beyond description. His commissions were placed with the great centres of the goldsmith's art, Augsburg, Nuremberg and Vienna. In addition most courts employed their own court jewellers (Ill. 115).

Jewels, even in the post-medieval period, were worn not only for their aesthetic appeal and monetary value. Right into the 18th century precious stones were thought to have magic powers. The emerald, for example, was said to strengthen the brain and, unbelievably, pearls and other precious stones were ground to a powder and taken orally for all sorts of diseases and chronic ailments. The stones which decorate pieces from the famous Cheapside Hoard (Ill. 114) cannot have been chosen haphazardly: chalcedony was widely used as an amulet and rubies were accorded magic powers. We may only glance briefly at the wealth of the material: a history of the goldsmith's craft could be written around the perfume flacon alone.

One of the earliest examples of a container which shows the transition from pomander to scent bottle is also one of the most splendid. Unfortunately, neither its maker nor owner are known to us. It was intended to be worn round the neck on a chain (Ill. 131).

There has been much speculation as to whether that genius of the Renaissance, Benvenuto Cellini (1500–1577) made or designed scent bottles. In his autobiography he speaks of medallions, seals, objects of all kinds, but of scent bottles there is no mention. His influence on the goldsmith's craft north of the Alps is, however, an acknowledged fact. Few definitive attributions, can be made concerning flacons of the 16th century; an exception is the gold repoussé scent bottle from the Prague court workshops (Ill. 115). Even bottles of the succeeding century in the main remain of unknown origin, bearing neither a master craftsman's signature nor a discharge mark. In the labyrinth of the art and antique trade knowledge of the original owner has often been lost. Anyone wishing to track down pieces by the great masters might be lucky if he visits one of the great treasure houses of Europe, the

Royal Collection in Rosenborg Castle in Copenhagen. There the real enthusiast for such small precious artefacts will derive satisfaction from the fact that they can be seen in the setting in which they were used, an almost totally unchanged environment, and moreover in chambers which attest to an unbroken monarchical tradition. Among countless small treasures, the collection possesses a number of fine scent bottles, including an admirable specimen in the form of a pilgrim's flask once owned by Christian V and his consort Queen Charlotte. And as if that were not enough it also has two of similar type, but each with a conical foot. These came from the workshop of one of the greatest German silversmiths and enamellers, Johann Melchior Dinglinger (1664–1731) who acquired his reputation after producing a coffee service in 1701, and who raised the art of metalwork to new heigths with his famous work for the Grüne Gewölbe in Dresden (Ill. 117). To remain in Denmark, we must not omit the silverwork from the late 17th to early 19th century already mentioned in the paragraphs dealing with smelling boxes. This output in silver includes very many scent bottles. These northern creations are chiefly distinguished from their counterparts in the rest of Europe by their eccentric designs (Ill. 91–95, 103–107).

Spanish craftsmanship in this respect is stylistically totally different again (Ill. 88, 156, 172).

The country which, in the 18th century, saw the cult of perfume reach a highpoint unequalled elsewhere produced flacons which are unsurpassed in their extravagance. By country one really means the Court of Versailles. At such a court, where a different perfume was ordained for every day, indeed for every time of day and every change of costume, and where the sanitary arrangements were so inadequate that the call of nature was sometimes answered behind the hangings of the staterooms and corridors, the need for perfume and its requisite containers was understandable. Without doubt the finest examples of the latter are to be found in the Houbigant Collection in Paris. There we can see, for example, a gold flacon combined with a watch, decorated in basse-taille enamelling. Its maker was Jean Baptiste François Cheret. Other great masters of their craft were Jacques Meyboon, who we can only represent here with a modest gold mount (Ill. 302), Martin Langlois, Charles Thomas Coutellier and Louis Joseph Prévot. Before such masterpieces (Ill. 86, 87, 118) were arrived at, a certain evolution had to take place: earlier flacons are still baroque in spirit and show the traditional pilgrim's flask shape (Ill. 128).

The happy marriage of gold and enamelling is supremely illustrated by small objects made in the 18th century, and naturally includes scent bottles of both French and English origin. A flacon from the Schwarzkopf Collection (Ill. 87) is entirely in the spirit of the Rococo and shows the asymmetry of design first seen in a candlestick by Maissonier in 1728.

Bacchus is a new theme in connection with perfume (Ill. 123); perhaps this flacon, of which there are several examples, was conceived during the savouring of a robust wine.

The contribution of German gold and silversmiths is more readily assessed from the illustrations than from a thousand words of prose. It is hard to believe that the extremely finely engraved and enamelled heartshaped bottle (Ill. 129) was intended for scent. The funereal aspect, so often apparent in German art of this period, and which is here so starkly depicted, seems to be in such shocking contrast with the sensual and joyous nature of the vessel's contents. Nevertheless, the overall impression of this example is of a restrained and elegant design in spite of the doleful message of its main motif, whereas the South German piece resembling a monstrance translated into the profane, so to speak, for all its craftsmanship has an appearance both disturbing and incorrect. (Ill. 119). This could also be said of the bottle attributed to a Magdeburg silversmith, with its interesting open-work overlaid casing (Ill. 120). It has a stiff and cold feeling about it, and there are indeed other examples of this kind of design (Ill. 144)

English craftsmen could stand up to comparison with their Continental counterparts. One would like to have seen the expression on the face of the builder who, one fine day in 1912, when working at a house in Cheapside, the main trading place of medieval London, unearthed a partly rotten casket with his pick axe and found that it contained no fewer than 243 valuable pieces of jewellery. They included gold chains, bracelets, rings, buttons, a watch, gemstones and various other items. Among them was a scent bottle of excellent quality and great value. Known as the Cheapside Hoard, all this treasure can be seen in the Museum of London and is perhaps the most important cache of buried treasure of this nature which has ever been unearthed in England, or indeed in Northern Europe. It is thought that it was probably the stock of a jeweller and/or pawnbroker. It was most likely buried shortly after 1600 but for unknown reasons, for the uncertain times of the Civil War, the Great Plaque, and the Fire were yet to come. It is of socio-historical importance since its size and variety give us an insight into one aspect of the lifestyle of the times of Elizabeth I and James I (Ill. 114).

The rich looking dressing table bottle, also dating from Elizabeth I's reign and, passing over four monarchs, the William & Mary (1689–1694) flacon decorated with symmetrical foliage decoration, demonstrate the equality of English craftsmanship with that of the Continent (Ill. 111, 113). Likewise the high quality of engraving is shown in the delicate, flat shouldered silver bottle in the Victoria and Albert Museum (Ill. 112).

In the 18th century French style was emulated by English craftsmen since it was the desired fashion in most stately homes throughout the land. In addition London was a centre of world trade and it was therefore important to attract foreign buyers to this market by offering them objects in vogue.

A favourite and successful design was the inclusion of a high quality glass bottle, which could have stood alone without this enhancement, in a golden cagework of rococo scrolls and foliage. (Ill. 90, 138, 139). Bottles in semi-precious stone were similarly encaged, as were toilet caskets and étuis. This type of cage work was not new: smelling bottles in ruby glass had already been encaged, probably in Augsburg. French goldsmiths had also practised this technique. The finest cagework in the British Isles came from the workshop of James Cox of London (active from 1757 to 1791). He was one of the finest makers of automata and worked principally for the East India Company, devising presents for eastern potentates. It is also probable, however, that many objects embellished in this manner were made in the workshops of Soho, on the outskirts of Birmingham.

The rococo element in English gold work was strongly influenced by the designs of the Frenchman Meissonier, especially in the asymmetrical rocaille motifs, and was mainly to be seen in repoussé gold watch cases. One of the greatest exponents of gold repoussé work was G. M. Moser, who began his career as a coppersmith in London in 1720. Many of his étuis, chatelaines and boxes are extant. It is hard to say who was responsible for the extremely fine examples of English bottles in glass and in semi-precious stone (Ill. 91, 300) since they are not signed, nor is there any documentation. The gold work in the doubtless most important piece of the period (Ill. 138) is not necessarily from the hand of James Cox himself. In contrast with the exuberant decoration of this smelling bottle which appears so un-English in character, the cagework piece (in Ill. 140) shows a certain restraint of design, especially in the classical central motif which only fits uncomfortably into its rococo frame (Ill. 140.)

Bottles set in filigree are rare. An excellent example of Eastern Mediterranean origin is in a private collection in Munich (Launert 1974, Fig. 149). Gold and silver filigree work was carried out in several widely separated regions, mainly in Spain, Portugal and Scandinavia, but also in some German workshops. The almost exclusively abstract patterns render attribution difficult.

In this connection mention must also be made of two bottles at first glance reminiscent of filigree but which are, strictly speaking, a mixture of cloisonné and filigree in foliate motifs.

Research into the origins of these bottles, which surface from time to time in the trade, has drawn a blank. The glass is undoubtedly English, as is the mass produced étui of one of them (Ill. 89).

Rock crystal (quartz) and other semi-precious stones, including chalcedony which is closely related to the former, were used in medieval times to make amulets, small vessels, reliquaries, dishes and other decorative objects. It was not until the Renaissance, however, that the art of cutting such materials came into its own, particularly throught the acquisition of new mineral sources overseas. Along with flint, rock crystal is one of the most widely distributed minerals occurring on the earth's surface or at a shallow levels. In Europe it is mainly found in the Alps, parts of Czechoslovakia and in the vicinity of Idar Oberstein in the Hunsrück region of Germany, and not surprisingly has been cut and converted into fine objects since Roman times. The alleged magic powers of rock crystal and its resulting uses have already been alluded to. It was extensively used to make flacons and other decorative pieces: a stroll through the Kunsthistorisches Museum in Vienna is proof enough of this. Evidence of the art of stone cutting in Germany is provided by the flacon category of artefacts alone (Ill. 119, 122, 124, 126). A delightful contrast is to be seen between the modest bottle reminiscent of a traditional brandy flask from the Fichtelgebirge (Ill. 141), and the richly decorated example which most probably comes from the possession of a nobleman (Ill. 126).

Chalcedony from Madagascar was imported into Europe during the Renaissance by seafaring Arab traders or by the Portuguese on the way back from India, and was available in large quantities. It was frequently used for ornamental items.

Lapis lazuli has always been considered one of the finest semi-precious stones in the jewellery trade (Ill. 134). It is assumed that the raw material came to Europe by various routes from Afghanistan where it had been worked for several thousand years.

Malachite was also used for bottles. A very beautiful piece of Russian origin is in a private collection in Munich.

Turquoise is found, as a decorative element on scent bottles either in its pure form or in ceramic imitation (Ill. 285); it comes either from Persia or Sinai. Other gems set on to scent bottles are garnets, rubies, opals and diamonds.

A material peculiar to England and mined in the county of Derbyshire is the so-called "Blue John". Easily worked, and with attractive striations and colour variations, it is represented by several bottles, some caged in gold. Fine boxes and toilet caskets were also made in it. The seams in Derbyshire are said to be nearing exhaustion. A masterpiece of English workmanship in mocha stone is illustrated in K. Foster's book (1966, Plate 85). It is set with rose diamonds and is encaged in gold. In the same book (Plate 83) there is a photograph of an extremely rare bottle in bloodstone (hematite).

Agate was used relatively frequently (Ill. 143) and the collector of Chinese snuff or scent bottles will be familiar with specimens in coral; they are, however, rare in European worksmanship (Ill. 136).

There are thousands of residents, cultured residents that is in the city of Berlin, who have never heard of Berlin iron jewellery, let alone seen any. The municipal museum, however, can boast a small collection of it. To see it en masse, however, and that thanks to Napoleon Bonaparte, one must visit the town of Rouen. Without delving into the origins of this unusual jewellery

("Gold gab ich für Eisen" – I gave gold for iron) which today is worth almost as much as the gold for which it was exchanged to raise money for financing the war against Napoleon, it must be noted that apart from jewellery as such, fans, watchstands, medals and indeed scent bottles are also found. The example of the latter illustrated here is, it is true, the only one the author has seen (Ill. 145). No less an artist than Karl Friedrich von Schinkel provided designs for Berlin iron jewellery.

Rosewater bottles and table ornament

Today the fingerbowl will probably contain water with a slice of lemon floating in it, or a dash of Eau de Cologne: in the post Middle Ages and into the 18th century it was customary to wash one's lips and hands with rosewater or something similar after eating, or to sprinkle the forehead and temples with it during the course of the meal. Every elegant table required the vessels necessary for this purpose and they were used communally by the guests. Such vessels formed part of a table service or were a suitable match for it. The simplest solution was the rosewater sprinkler but in aristocratic circles it had to be a perfume fountain which, in all its glory, became the centrepiece of the dining table (Ill. 154). Each guest was not infrequently provided with a silver or gold dish.

In 16th and 17th century England the "casting bottle" or "scent flaggon" was used. It differed from the later scent bottles only in size and in the possession of a perforated lid; spray bottles were also known. Queen Elizabeth had no fewer than three such bottles. A particularly splendid example, with decoration from the pattern book containing designs by Hans Holbein for silverware for Henry VIII, came on to the market a short time ago (Ill. 111). It was probably a New Year's gift which a fishmonger by the name of Foster made for Queen Mary in 1587. A similar bottle but taller (170 mm) and with a silver weigth of 150 g, dating from 1563, and probably from the hand of the same craftsman, is to be seen in L. Matthew's book (1973).

In English literature of the time of Shakespeare to the sprinkling of head, face and hands lead us to believe that rosewater sprinklers were not only used at the dining but also at the dressing table.

Perfume manufacturers of today are hardly likely to consider a material other than glass to contain their product. There are some modern porcelain bottles, it is true, and metal is occasionally used, mainly for atomisers. Years ago a firm in Grasse sold a perfume in an aluminium flacon, the advantage of this

BOTTLES IN UNUSUAL MATERIALS OR MODELLED ON THEMES FROM NATURE metal being its lightness and unbreakable nature, but it was unpleasing to the eye, especially after long use.

In collections of bottles from earlier centuries materials other than glass, porcelain and precious metal are thinly represented. Stoneware is not very suitable for several reasons. The main objection is probably of aesthetic and psychological origin, for there exists a mental association between it and its common function as tankard, jug or jar. The material is too coarse and linked with its cheap and ordinary contents. Faults in the glaze, even the tiniest crack, would damage the valuable perfume contens or lead to its evaporation It may consequently be assumed that the few small stoneware flasks extant were in fact smelling bottles. The pocket watch bottle (Ill. 188) has a twin in Hove Museum and two very interesting earlier specimens of scent bottles in this humble material, dating from 1740, are to be seen in the collections at Stoke-on-Trent. All the examples mentioned are in brown salt glazed stoneware. As interesting as it is rare is a much later example from the firm of Doulton (Ill. 189).

Alabaster has seldom been used, being too soft and friable. At the same time thin walled bottles made of it can, owing to their transparency, look extremely attractive: this is demonstraded by an excellent piece in a private collection in Munich (Launert 1974, Fig. 197).

Amber possesses qualities which virtually preclude its use for scent bottles. It is brittle and tends to develop hairline cracks, allowing contents to evaporate. It is also possible that it would react chemically with certain perfume ingredients, being itself a resinous substance, a semi-fossil, in fact. There are only a few flacons, admittedly including some superb specimens, in this mysterious yellow-brown or golden substance (Ill. 166, 167).

Even rarer, and just as unsuitable for scent bottles, is ivory. The extensive literature on this animal product makes no mention of scent bottles, but the Kunstgewerbemuseum in West Berlin possesses several extremely finely carved examples (Ill. 163–165). The Schwarzkopf Collection can also boast an ivory scent bottle (Ill. 161) but neither this nor the others has a documented history. The fine carved specimen with a figure of a young lady on its reverse was probably a wedding gift (Ill. 165). Among the less well known and, from the artistic point of view, less important ivory bottles, a turned piece is occasionally found, usually in the form of a bee hive.

The centre of ivory carving in the 17th and early 18th century was the town of Dieppe. Of all the objects known to have been made there, none are scent bottles, but there is evidence of smelling boxes (Ill. 109).

There is a material which is often deceptively like ivory but which comes from the plant rather than the animal kingdom. Much more difficult to work than real ivory, it comes from the endosperm of the seed of South American palms belonging to the genus Phytelephas, is ivory coloured, very hard and of uniform structure. In the past it was very important to the button industry but it was subsequently replaced by synthetic materials. This palm seed, traded as vegetable ivory, coroso or tagua, was transformed into all sorts of souvenir items, and it is to this category that the fairly common, almost egg-shaped, bottles belong. They were most probably sold at fairs. The nut was hollowed out, the seed coat removed, the surface polished and treated with a reddish or greenish colouring agent. The closure consists usually of a simple screw.

There is no area of interest for a collector which is without its surprises. No-one would imagine that wood had ever been used for the making of scent bottles, yet one inevitably comes across several examples in this universal and gratifyingly workable material when investigating a major collection. In some cases it is merely the outer casing of a neatly fitting glass bottle, in others a nutshaped artistically pierced holder into which the perfume container (a glass tube) is inserted. Then there are the true wooden scent bottles (Ill. 158–160). Only very fine grained hard woods are suitable for this purpose (Ill. 159, 160). Ebony bottles often have inlaid ivory decorations to provide an attractive contrast of materials. These wooden bottles would hardly be used for a modern perfume, unless as a throwaway novelty, for bottles in even the hardest woods would have irregularities on the inside, allowing traces of perfume to cling and thus tainting a refill of a different fragrance.

Tortoiseshell, mentioned elsewhere concerning etuis, was seldom used for flacons. It is extremely difficult to make hollow containers from this substance which can only be worked when warm. The exquisite example in illustration 168 must therefore be considered a rarity.

In the Far East countless snuff bottles were made from coral, yet scent bottles are all but non-existent in this wonderful natural product. It is, therefore, all the more exciting to be able to show in this book a masterpiece of puzzling provenance (Ill. 136).

Man was able to avail himself of natural forms and materials for his purposes long before he devised vessels in pottery or metal. The ox or buffalo horn immediately comes to mind, or the mammoth tusk, all used as storage or drinking vessels. Fakirs today eat their meals from large nutshells or similar bowls and pilgrims on their way to Mecca are only allowed to eat from dishes made from natural substances. It is a sign of civilisation, however, when such objects not only exist in their simple form for daily use, but are also ornamented. The earliest drawings of drinking horns show examples with silver and gold mounts. King Harold's, as seen in the Bayeux Tapestry, must have been a particularly beautiful specimen, decorated as it was at tip and mouth.

Vessels of all kinds made from tusks, shells, nuts, or even hooves, have come down to us from the Middle Ages, but the greatest variety came at the

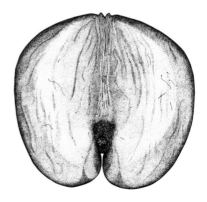

Fig. 24 Coco-de-mer or sea coconut (Lo-doicea maldivica)

46

time of the Renaissance, at that time of exploration and discovery when exotic objects were brought to Europe from the four quarters of the globe, exciting the imagination of the goldsmiths of the day. The iconography of the coconut alone (*Cocos nucifera*), first brought back from Asia by Portuguese seafarers, could fill a book. In this category is the legendary Seychelles palm nut (*Lodoicea maldivica*), a curiosity par excellence (Fig. 24). First properly identified by western science in the 18th century, it also went under the name of coco-de-mer, the heaviest and largest fruit in the plant kingdom, weighing up to 18 kg. As flotsam it was known long ago on the coasts of the Indian Ocean and was as prized as ambra so that owning it was the prerogative of the rulers of that part of the world. Seafarers brought it to Europe in the early 16th century and it was much sought after by kings and princes. It is reported that Emperor Rudolf II paid no fewer than 4000 gilders for a single specimen. It is obvious that a person who could afford such a sum would also have the means to embellish his trophy. In the history of perfume containers the perfume fountain in Ill. 154 is hardly to be outdone in majesty and splendour.

Other unusual materials include fruits of the gourd family and countless types of shell, from the cowrie to the large snail of the genus *Conus* and its kin. An additional factor in the case of shells is the symbolic intention (cf. p. 22) and the fact that not only are the shells themselves used, but are imitated in other materials (Ill. 66, 97). Particularly favoured and often featured in medieval and later painting – in the works of Botticelli, for example – are the great scallop *(Pecten maximum)* and the St. James shell or fan shell *(Pecten jacobaeus)* (Fig. 3, Ill. 279).

The many Roman scent containers shaped like shells which have survived are noteworthy. The most beautiful of these are the mould-blown examples in the Römisch-Germanisches Museum in Cologne and certain similar pieces in the British Museum (Fig. 3). Mention must also be made of the shell-shaped toilet dishes and handbasins in faience and porcelain, especially those made in Delft in the 17th and 18th centuries. As far as scent bottles go, the shell shape is surprisingly common (Ill. 254, 279). The swan mussel (Anadonta), and particularly the river mussel (Margaratifera), were widely used as the many charming 19th century examples show (Ill. 170). Here the two natural shells are cleverly held together by a brass or pinchbeck brace. Shells were also converted into boxes in similar fashion. Judging by the large number of these flacons in the cheaper range which have survived they must have been extremely popular. Whether they were actually functional is unsure. The shell motif is also found, highly stylised, in much silverwork. In their natural form sea shells were an ideal material for the scent bottle maker; tastefully mounted they are nature improved upon. These flacons too, almost always from the firm of S. Mordan, must have found an eager market.

The plant kingdom also yields natural forms which, on account of their pleasing shape, fitting comfortably into the palm of the hand, are often turned into scent bottles, as specimens made from nuts show.

Whoever had the ingenuity to convert peach stones into scent bottles is unknown. His creations all have a daintily turned ivory stopper or screw insertion. Even the walnut (*Juglans regia*) was an inspiration, especially in the second half of the 19th century, but in this case we are speaking of imitations in silver and porcelain for scent bottles and etuis, the nut itself being rarely used (Ill. 332). Its symbolism was by now long forgotten but is dealt with on page 20. The lemon shaped scent bottle is a rare item.

As far as motifs are concerned, a cursory flick through the illustrated pages of this book is enough to reveal that the higher animal kingdom is richly represented. One could build up a veritable menagerie of bottles in the shape of various animals. From fish, to reptiles, to the big cats, hardly a group is not represented; indeed even the human form is there.

ENAMEL FLACONS

Finely ground glass, metal oxides to give colour, and a flux are prerequisites for the process of enamelling. The practice of this ancient art, first mentioned in 240 B.C., has evolved four different techniques: champlevé, cloisonné, basse-taille and enamel painting. The champlevé technique involves filling enamelling troughs cut into the metal surface with the powdered enamel mixture and then fusing it in the kiln. When the cooling process is completed the surface is filed, then smoothed with pumice, crocus powder and rouge. This technique was seldom employed for scent bottles (Ill. 88). In cloisonné enamelling, cells are formed on the metal surface by soldering on metal wires. These cells are then similarly filled with the enamel mixture. This type of enamelling can be seen in scent containers, especially Brûle-Parfums (Ill. 131, 172); the plique-à-jour process is not of interest here – briefly, it is a mosaic-like cloisonné method, but without a metal ground, and is chiefly employed by jewellers. The much finer basse-taille technique, dating from the 14th century, was also rarely used for scent bottles. It demands great artistic skill, since the design being aimed at must be cut into the metal surface, the resulting hollows of different depths having then been filled with translucent enamel mixtures in previous centuries. It was usually applied to liturgical vessels. The great masters of this technique were the French. It enjoyed a revival at one point and a few years ago an early 19th century flacon with this form of decoration came on to the market (Launert 1974, Plate XVII).

With reference to perfume containers we are mainly concerned with enamel painting, the least ancient of the techniques. It was probably developed, as were so many new processes, in 16th century Venice. The surface of a metal object was covered with a uniform film of enamel, this providing a vehicle for the painting which could be executed in mono- or polychrome. Initially the main problem with this process was to make sure that the enamel layer successfully adhered to the metal, since the two materials have different ratios of expansion so that, during cooling, tensions are created resulting in cracks. A solution to the problem was soon found, especially for thin metal, namely that of coating both sides of the plate with enamel. There is a very interesting scent bottle in the form of an articulated fish which is of Venetian origin (Ill. 174). In the 16th century Limoges had established itself as the centre of European enamelling, but it is unlikely that scent bottles were made there. It was not until the 17th century that the art of enamelling was practised in all countries north of the Alps.

It was in the nature of things that enamelling was in the hands of gold an silversmiths, although watchmakers or, more correctly, watchcase makers, mastered the technique to perfection as can be seen in any of our important horological collections. A fine example of the dual function of watch and scent bottle, from a French workshop, may be seen in illustration 116. It is often impossible to ascribe pieces of this period to a particular workshop since signatures are seldom found on them. Only by comparing objects of all kinds known to have come from certain centres may one have a stab at possible provenance. A certain kind of flower decoration, even when consisting solely of tulips, does not have to be of Dutch origin. The rustic style of painting recalling that on Dutch faience, which is to be seen on the delightful heart-shaped flacon in illustration 173, makes the attribution in this case fairly safe.

Anyone who has spent long years tramping the corridors of European museums, viewing at great auction houses, browsing in antique shops and gaining access to private collections will have noticed that bottles of this period seldom have doubles.

From the beginning they were made as unique items, or at least their doubles have been lost in the course of time. The most excellent pieces were probably private commissions. Could not the heart, already mentioned, in illustration 173 have served as a betrothal gift? Its painted decoration resembles, both in style and technique, that of the superior example in illustration 179. This latter bottle is set in a garnet encrusted silver band, possibly from the same silversmith as the former, and indeed a double of it is known. Differing from both in shape and the quality of the mount, although with an orientally inspired decoration, the flacon in the shape of a double gourd could be of Dutch or German origin. By comparing it with a piece in its original leather étui which appeared a short while ago at auction, and which was signed by its maker, the noble bottle in Ill. 135 could be attributed to a London goldsmith, Aaron Barting, who called himself a "smallworker in gold", and who had established a shop at 112 St. Martin's Street, from which address on February 14, 1775 he insured his brick building for £ 400, its contents for £ 50 and his clothing for £ 50.

The close association of goldsmith and enameller – the work was not necessarily always done by one person – is most evident in bottles with enamel insets. Much enamelling was done by itinerant craftsmen who knew where the need was and often found employment, apprentice fashion, taking up residence in the master's household. The naive spontaneity of such insets (Ill. 118, 129) has its roots in folk art and resembles the contemporary paintings of saints made for the peasant home. The decorative themes of these two bottles probably indicate that they were wedding presents.

In the 18th century, that last flowering of a unified European culture, that epoch of elegance and extravagance of zest for living during which perfume began to play an increasing, eventually excessive, part, the picture changes dramatically. For the gentry of the rococo, beautiful things for the decoration of the person and the enhancement of the environment were the tangible manifestation of an exuberant lifestyle which, superficially at least, seemed totally divorced from daily cares. Precious metals and costly jewels dominated the age which knew itself to be golden, and had a function not only in its profane but also in its sacred areas. Churches and monasteries of that era – one only has to think of the Wieskirche in the Allgäu – are a testimony to the way in which the spirit of the rococo penetrated and pervaded the religious life.

But apart from the highest in the land there were other social strata whose needs had to be satisfied, so we see gold or gilded metals being used in combination with cheaper materials such as tortoiseshell, mother-of-pearl, porcelain, ivory and, of course, enamel. Thus the range of artistic possibilities was increased, and the materials could be used to create contrast, thereby heightening the dramatic and artistic effect of an object. The technique of enamelling allowed copper sheeting to be used instead of gold, which it was a waste to hide anyway; thus the required effect was obtained at a lower cost. Enamelled ware had an economic advantage over porcelain too, being cheaper to produce, and it was possible to guarantee a steady supply for an eager market by producing blanks which could be decorated and assembled when there was a demand. In addition, it was less likely to get broken. Today, of course, we can see from extant pieces that the danger of damage lay at the edges of the object, where the enamel meets the mount, or, in the case of ornamentation in relief, on protruding surfaces.

In German-speaking Europe two main centres of enamelling had been established in the 17th century, namely Augsburg and Berlin, both reaching their zenith in the course of the 18th. Unfortunately it is impossible to attribute even one scent bottle of German provenance to a particular workshop in the town made famous by the Fuggers (Ill. 80, 129), but we fare better in the case of Berlin. Here we know of one of the many Hugenot émigrés without whom the cultural life of the city would have been much the poorer, Pierre Fromery. An engraver and gunsmith from Sedan, he was made court armourer to the Elector and founded a so-called quincaillerie, a workshop for the manufacture and distribution of haberdashery which over the years developed into a major business handling the production of orders and insignia – Fromery had the monopoly for Prussian army uniform buttons! – as well as weapons. After his death the firm was carried on by his son Alexander, who evidently had inherited little of his father's business ability but who was responsible for a wealth of extraordinarily fine enamelled objects, particularly boxes of all kinds. Many of them, naturally, were vehicles for the glorification of proud Prussia. An indication of enamel's advantage over porcelain, including the speed at which it can be produced, is a box decorated with a scene from the Battle of Leuthen during the Seven Year War (5. 12. 1757) with a manufacturing date of precisely one week later. Alexander Fromery employed the best enamel craftsman of the day, Christoph Conrad Hunger, who will be mentioned later (cf. p. 56), and the enamel painter Johann Herold, as research by the German art historian A. Drier has shown. Chreations from Fromery's workshops differ from the rest of contemporary production in their silvered or gilded relief decoration which is often applied as cartouches or single elements in the flower decoration. On close inspection of these decorative motifs, and noticing the repetition of certain details, we may conclude that these silver and gold reliefs were formed in moulds and applied to the enamelled surface (Ill. 177). Further conclusions may be drawn from a comparison of this relief decoration with patterns already used by C. C. Hunger when he was working for the Meissen Porcelain Manufacture (Ill. 200). Two Fromery bottles, considered to be his finest, are in the Houbigant Collection in Paris, one of which is distinguished from all other bottles in this category by its extremely carefully worked gold setting. The typical relief decoration on the modest bottle in the shape of a gourd (Ill. 80) would also indicate its Fromery origin. Attribution is often made difficult owing to the fact that Fromery bought ready made bottles from Augsburg for enamelling in his workshops, and to complicate matters further, "Hausmaler", freelance painters working from home, were often contracted to do the work (cf. p. 56).

In artistic and cultural matters of taste the 18th century was subject to two influences: the French, which penetrated into the very speech of Central European courts, and the English, which pervaded the northern states. Our subject shows two exceptions to this general tendency: the English enamel flacons and china scent bottles (Ill. 229–244) appear, compared with items of glass or furniture of the period, so un-English that one would assume them to be the products of Gallic culture.

There is no simple explanation for this phenomenon. It is true that the Chelsea Porcelain Factory was founded by a Fleming and a Frenchman and that many foreigners, chiefly Germans and Frenchmen (in 1759 a committee report from the House of Commons mentions no fewer than 30–40 foreign craftsmen and artists), brought their own style into enamel production, but in the final analysis foreign influence was no guarantee that the wares would be acceptable to the public, and England has always been noted for its reluctance to abandon its own ideas on matters of taste. Nevertheless, there was a marked tendency among the higher levels of society under the Hanoverian rulers to imitate things French. The ultimate form the rococo took on the Continent never, however, crossed the English Channel. There is another explanation for the French style of manufactured items: the English, cynically referred to as 'a nation of shopkeepers' by Napoleon, had, with their cool instinct, discovered a foreign market which needed satisfying and a large part of the enamel and china production was intended for export. This trade flourished until the continental blockade put an end to it at the time of Napoleon. Its temporary success, however, may be judged from the fact that the Prussian government felt it necessary to impose import duty on English enamel ware.

'Battersea' is a term often seen on museum labels and bandied about in the antique trade referring to English export enamels. In fact very few pieces, and certainly no scent bottles, came from this factory which was founded by Stephen Jansen in 1752 on the south bank of the Thames, and which was only in operation for three years. As has been proved, the majority of enamel ware, including all scent bottles, came from Staffordshire, the most important centres being Bilston, Birmingham and Wednesbury. By mid-century so many small items such as scent bottles, boxes, bonbonnières, seals and so on were being made that Birmingham was known as the 'toyshop of Europe', "toy" being used here in the sense of trinket or bauble. Having said this, on account of both shape and decoration the bottle in Ill. 183 may be of a London provenance around 1765. In the Birmingham area alone there were no fewer than six enamel factories. It may be assumed that here, at the heart of the English metal industry, a division of labour took place whereby one firm pressed the metal and another undertook its embellishment. Not all painters were employed permanently by a particular firm, but rather were employed for a particular series, often changing from one manufacture to another or working for several simultaneously. There are sometimes cases when one can recognise the hand of more than one artist on an object, but it is impossible to attribute anything to any particular person, any particular factory or indeed any particular place, on account of the lack of signatures. For the enthusiast of these delightful items this frustration of scholarly instinct is of minor importance. It is more interesting to consider the sources of the painted decoration. Faced with a vast number of enamel bottles, and the same can be said of porcelain smelling bottles, such as the Schreiber collection in the Victoria and Albert Museum in London, or those in the

British Museum, one cannot fail to be surprised by the lack of original design on the part of the painters. In the V. & A. this is underlined when we look at a nearby exhibit, a vase decorated by Pablo Picasso, then turn to our, rococo enamels with their painted decoration forming a veritable gallery of reproductiones of the works of French painters from Watteau to Nattier and showing engravings by François Ravenet, P. Avelline and others (Ill. 176, 178, 183, 184l).

Some bottles show portraits, the best known being that of Lady Fenhoulet after the painting by Sir Joshua Reynolds (the same portrait appears on a box in the Schreiber Collection). Others have allegorical themes taken from mezzotints, as, for example, "The Seasons" by Richard Houston. Among the engravers employed for enamel and metal manufacture, the most famous is a Frenchman, Simon François Ravenet (1706–1774). Next to him in importance is Robert Hancock, mainly an imitator, who later was in charge of painting at the Worcester China Factory. A less known enamel painter was Abraham Seemann, a German who, like many of his countrymen, settled in Birmingham; it is not sure whether he worked on scent bottles. Flowers and birds (Ill. 180, 184 m) are taken from contemporary lavishly illustrated books on botanical and zoological themes (we know for certain that the Chelsea Porcelain Factory used the plant drawings of that great German illustrator, G. D. Ehret). Relatively rare are landscapes (Ill. 184 l) and harbour scenes (Ill. 183) which are depicted in paintings and prints of the periods.

Given that all these painted decorations are copies from other sources, we cannot but admire the skill and sensitivity with which these unknown artists, for very little financial reward, translated masterpieces of painting and engraving into miniature form and adapted them to the curving surface of the flacons.

One category of enamelled scent bottles is decorated with transfer prints. An Irishman by the name of John Brooks is credited with the introduction of this technique. He attempted to have his invention patented in Birmingham in September 1751, but was unsuccessful. He was later the director of the short-lived Battersea Manufacture. Unless a further overpainting was done, however, the print decoration was rather feeble looking, as can be seen on the few boxes which have survived in this state. Scent bottles without the overpainting are extremely rare.

As far as shape is concerned – most scent bottles have the pleasing teardrop shape already familiar on the Continent – enamel bottles from English and other manufactures are certainly in imitation of continental porcelain ones. It might be argued, that this shape is the best one for perfume bottles anyway.

Even when flacon and box were combined, the inspiration came from Meissen and other continental manufacturers. The imitation of shapes in porcelain was mainly on economic grounds; the aim was to undercut competitors in porcelain. If we are to judge by the large number of enamelled items, this strategy was successful until the political initiatives already mentioned, and the uncertainties of war, put paid to everything.

As stated above, enamelling was mostly executed by the goldsmiths. This would account for the fact that the technique was restricted to small objects. Small they may be, but enamel scent bottles would not have been accorded such prominence in our museums, nor fired the literary imagination, if they were not also the most charming and daintiest containers in the history of scent. In spite of the technical problems of enamelling on a larger scale, there are two categories of objects which are exceptions to the tendency to make only small items in enamelled ware, namely candlesticks and brûle-parfums. In their function both are exposed to heat, to the element fire, to which 18th century glass and porcelain were less adapted. Candlesticks of outstanding beauty have survived but enamelled perfume burners are rare. A superb Staffordshire example in the form of an urn on a plinth, almost 25 cm high, dating from 1775, was auctioned in London several years ago. It has a light blue ground delicately decorated with raised floral sprays, and, in a rocaille cartouche a freely painted landscape which is not to be found on scent bottles of the period. Potential buyers of Staffordshire enamel bottles must be warned that they were also produced by that industrious maker of imitations, Emile Samson of Paris (cf. p. 60).

The making of enamel wares came to an end in England as the century faded, as indeed it did in Germany. Only in France, Vienna and Geneva did the art revive spasmodically in the 19th century. The results were only imitative and nowhere did the technique enjoy a development of new style (Ill. 186, 187).

The scent bottle enthusiast cannot fail, however, to be excited by a group of costly ingenious toys – for that is what they are – scentbottle automata (Ill. 182). Finally, the coup de grâce is symbolically given to European enamelling by the perfume pistol (Ill. 185) in the Musée Cognac-Jay in Paris. It was probably made by the Swiss firm of Jaquet-Droz in the 19th century.

Meissen   PORCELAIN FLACONS

Porcelain, or china, is the queen of ceramics. It is impervious, translucent white, hard as iron, heat and acid resistant and an ideal vehicle for painted decoration. Given the correct proportions of the necessary ingredients, it is obtained by heating kaolin (white china clay), which on it own will not fuse, with chinastone or petuntse (a feldspathic mineral composed of silicate of potassium and aluminium) which will, to a temperature of between 1250 and 1350° C. The resulting product, known as hard porcelain or pâte dure, had

Fig. 25   "The sense of smell", one of a series of figures representing the five senses. Painted porcelain. Modelled by Joseph Nees, Zurich, c. 1770. H. 163 mm. MKG/CB

been known in China since the 7th or 8th century, and in the course of its long history there works of art were created which few Western countries can match for their finesse. It was Marco Polo who was the first European to see the "white gold" in the 13th century, and who presumably brought some specimens back to the West.

The limited quantity of porcelain which was imported into Europe in the Middle Ages was highly valued in aristocratic circles. The earliest complete item extant is a Seladon dish with a richly gilded mount executed by a German goldsmith. It is in the Landesmuseum in Cassel and must have been brought over around 1440. The ever increasing amount subsequently arriving in the West was not only destined for the treasuries of European princes but served as model and inspiration for our ceramic industry. It led to repeated attempts to discover the secret of porcelain making which for centuries had been the closely guarded secret of the Chinese.

These attempts led to an important development in Venetian glassmaking, namely milk glass, a product ressembling porcelain to some extent. Nearer the mark was the manufacture of the first western porcelain at the Medici factory in Florence between 1575 and 1587 and later in France (c. 1680); it was not, however, true porcelain, but so called soft paste porcelain or pâte tendre, made by melting down several materials at low temperatures, mainly white clay and ground glass. It was nevertheless of some consequence, because it later became the sole product of certain English and French factories.

The veil of secrecy was finally lifted when true porcelain was made by the eminent scientist and scholar Ehrenfried Walter von Tschirnhaus assisted by Johann Friedrich Böttger, a gifted alchemist of dubious character. From this discovery came the foundation of the Meissen Porcelain Factory in 1710, chiefly thanks to the passion the King of Saxony, Augustus the Strong had for collecting porcelain. Its resounding success is a piece of history which cannot be recounted here. Among the marvellous creations which saw the ligth there under the supervision of Johann Gregor Hörold and, later, Johann Joachim Kändler, there were in fact only a few scent bottles along with other minor but delightful items such as bonbonnières, snuff boxes, cane handles, and necessaires. In the volume of literature on the subject of Meissen, scent bottles are given only a footnote, so to speak, and even well preserved factory archives give little information about them, as an inquiry proved. No wonder that the factory's archivist in his monumental history of the factory does not show one scent bottle. And yet bottles are to be found in museum and private collections from every period of the firm's existence. Larger objects such as pot-pourri vases and perfume burners were produced and are documented.

In line with all other objects made during Meissen's early years, perfume containers mimic the Chinese imports. This is most obvious in the case of brûle-parfums in the form of sitting buddhas, called, curiously enough, pagodas (in the factory archives also "Bajoden") (Ill. 34). The oldest example of these awesome figures was made in Böttger porcelain i. e. porcelain of the early period made of kaolin, alabaster or chalk and quarz. The most exotic example, made after 1715, is in the Dresden Porcelain Collection; it shows a grinning buddha with half open mouth, his stomach naked to below the navel, in an altar-like – or fireplace-like – porcelain surround which is decorated with masks of women and lions and formal floral decoration. Scent bottles are not easy to date and it is only possible by comparing them stylistically with other objects. It would seem that none were made before 1730. Among the earliest were probably those in illustrations 191 and 192, which in shape and decoration have a Far Eastern air about them. This influence is even more evident in the bottles painted in the Kakiemon style, so called after a Japanese artist of that name. Similar bottles are in the Schneider Collection in Schleißheim near Munich where, as well as the red dragon motif (Ill. 193), the yellow tiger is also to be seen.

Not until Kaendler's engagement by the factory in 1731 did the most important period in the history begin, and with it the departure from the Far Eastern style of scent bottle. The rocaille bottle in illustration 195 strongly recalls the silver work of the rococo. This bottle must have been a very popular one for we meet with it not only in several versions in Meissen, but also in the production of rival firms, and in a less elegant form it was made at the factory in St. Petersburg.

A rarity is the flacon painted with so-called "Goldchinesen" (Ill. 194). This style of painting is thought to have been done by the "Hausmaler", that is, free lance painters working outside the factory. Among the most important of these artists were Bartholomäus Seuter in Augsburg and his fellow resident Johannes Auffenwerth, a goldsmith. Whether this bottle may be attributed to the Augsburg painters is uncertain because the most recent view is that in later years this gold painting, which wore off easily, by the way, was also done on the factory premises. The objects from which the idea for such painting came are in the Japanese Palace in Dresden where Augustus the Strong housed the great collection of Japanese porcelain which he had been collecting since 1717. This included many pieces from the hands of the Kakiemon family of artists who set the style for such things in the Japanese province of Arita in the 17th century.

A totally different type of gold decoration was the so-called appliqué enamelling, developed in Meissen by the highly talented itinerant enameller C. C. Hunger around 1715. Pieces decorated by him are extremely rare.

Unfortunately the bottle in illustration 203, in form and style still totally in the spirit of the baroque, is an imitation of one of his pieces, albeit an excellent one, by the firm of Samson in Paris. It nevertheless gives us a good idea of how the original must have been, or is, if extant. Some of the simplest but most attractive Meissen flacons deserve a passing glance: the elliptical bottles which show a landscpae or flower decoration in a reserve, while the rest of the surface displays the so-called Altozier pattern. This pattern, recalling wickerwork, is usually almost always restricted to the rims of plates.

Statuette bottles from the Meissen craftsmen do not compare in quantity and variety with the Chelsea ones dealt with later, and are lacking in originality compared with those of other German factories. They are at all events relatively rare. The commedia dell'arte figures, especially Harlequin, reflect the genius of their creator, Johann Joachim Kändler (Ill. 214). The basis for the designs for all the figures, and bottles, in this group are the copper engravings by Callot, and Watteau's paintings, but Kändler did not slavishly copy them. Widely distributed, often copied, and made continuously into the 19th century is a bottle in the form of a Capuchin friar who is trying to smuggle a girl hidden in a sheaf of corn into a monastery (Ill. 215). One can well imagine the effect this amusing and relatively harmless piece must have had in the anti-Catholic atmosphere of 18th century England. This figure too has its origins in an engraving, namely one by John Bowles dating from 1760 entitled "Provender for the Monastery". A critical article by De Coo in 1984 established that the engraving itself was a flagrant act of print piracy. The author traces the theme back to its source and attempts to interpret its underlying motives. Its translation into porcelain probably had less profound motifs. As well as the above mentioned scent bottles, Meissen produced some in the form of fruits. In the course of the 19th century some bottles were produced at the factory which is still, incidentally in production today. The 19th century specimen in illustration 258 is in the style of the rococo, but lacks the artistic authenticity of the period as well as its lightness, elegance and genius. Its basic sensual appeal does not need pointing out. More convincing is the same piece in a private collection. In this example the drop-like stopper in the form of a yellowish-brown rose bud forms a logical whole with the rest of the design, completing the erotic symbolism. The modelling makes it clear that the young lovers will not resist temptation. The continued production of models of the factory's "great" period has damaged its reputation, especially when modellers and painters who were not equal to the task of recreating them in the spirit of the original were employed. It remains unclear to what extent the need for mass production, and there must have been a lively market for such wares, contributed to this decline.

Meissen of the Neo-classical or Marcolini period, the latter term deriving from the name of the factory director in charge from 1774 to 1814, is represented here by a noble, clean lined, first rate scent bottle (Ill. 256). The same model, by chance in the same collection, is shown in Ill. 255, but it has painted decoration in rococo style.

The two mid 19th century bottles in Ill. 263, 264 in the Biedermeier style have a Meissen attribution. They were most certainly designed for the dressing table. In their shape, and indeed in their stopper design, both closely resemble glass bottles of their time. If the upper part of the white flacon did not have applied flower decoration it could be taken for a pressed glass imitation. The literature on 19th century Meissen production is much more limited than that on the great period: descent on to a plain is much less exciting than ascent to a mountain peak, after all. It is therefore difficult to place this interesting piece. One could, however, risk attributing it to Ernst August Leuteritz himself or to his influence by comparing it with other items having the same pressed glass effect – as shown markedly on a vase in the form of a chalice (mould number I/86) and by the design for a cup in the late Gothic style in the Meissen archives. Our last Meissen piece is a bottle which in form and style is a bit of a mishmash (Ill. 265). The pâte-sur-pâte technique used here, already practised in ancient China, was revived at Sèvres in the mid-19th century. Meissen did not take it up until 1878. Its main exponents there were Konrad Hentschel and Theodor Grust. One cannot attribute this bottle to either one of them (with certainty). The pâte-sur-pâte technique requires a high degree of skill: several layers are superimposed, creating a low relief decoration which permits the ground to shine through in delicate shades. Both of the above mentioned artists have given us some very fine examples of this work.

Other European factories

Maintaining the secrecy of the porcelain formula soon became impossible: disloyal employees absconded with the knowledge often in very adventurous circumstances, and as the second half of the century got underway porcelain factories were being set up in many small German towns and in most countries. It is impossible to give an account of all these manufactures within the confines of this book, with the exception of Chelsea, which flourished as a result of destruction at Meissen caused by the Prussian invasion of the year 1756. Most factories made scent bottles, and many of them, especially those in full rococo style, outdo the Meissen ones in originality and charm. It must be understood that, there being no such things as patents, not only was the formula for porcelain manufacture hawked around, but also the designs and indeed the actual moulds. This would explain why certain bottles, for example the monk-smuggling-girl piece and that with wicker decoration, are met with in various factories, including Chelsea.

The finest scent bottles which show no influence from Meissen or other factories were made in Vienna, the oldest hard porcelain factory after Meissen. It was founded in 1719 by Claude Innocentius du Paquier in collaboration with C. C. Hunger and Samuel Stölzel, both refugees from Meissen. Some of these flacons have fine relief ornamentation (Ill. 201, 202,

204); others show Schwarzlot painting, a form of decoration we shall later see on glass bottles. The effect of the Schwarzlot against the white porcelain is very charming.

Some delightful scent bottles were made in Kloster Veilsdorf in Thuringia. The commedia dell' arte is the inspiration for most of them (Ill. 216), but the goatherd and billygoat motif which we shall meet again in connection with other manufactures is especially pleasing. Like almost all the German princes, Ludwig VIII of Hessen-Darmstadt was also gripped by porcelain fever. He took over the Königstätten factory founded in 1758 and moved it to Kelterbach where, however, it survived for a mere seven years. The quality of the porcelain produced there differs from that of other manufactures in having a greyish tinge to it. All scent bottles from this factory have a certain unashamed crudity, yet the faces on the figures have incredibly lively expressions. These bottles were probably from the hand of the factory's chief modeller, Karl Vogelmann (Ill. 219, 223).

We can only mention scent bottles from the Fulda factory of the Princebishop Heinrich von Bibra; they are never seen. Fürstenberg, the manufacture founded in 1747 within the domain of Duke Karl of Brunswick, is on the other hand, well represented in collections as far as scent bottles are concerned. They are mainly in the form of typical elegant rococo people (Ill. 211), commedia dell'arte figures, or fruits, the latter often mistakenly referred to as Chelsea (Ill. 210). The Meissen bottle with wicker decoration was also copied.

Ludwigsburg was founded in 1760. The patron of this factory, which is considered second rate by connoisseurs, was one of the most enlightened and admirable absolute rulers of his day, Duke Karl Eugen von Württemberg. He had such keen enthusiasm for porcelain that he personally visited the Sèvres and Wedgwood factories. Ludwigsburg bottles (Ill. 222) are attributed to the modeller Johann Christian Wilhelm Beyer.

Nymphenburg, founded in 1761 just outside the city walls of Munich, unfortunately produced no scent bottles in the great period. What a fantastic contribution Franz Anton Bustelli, that genius of porcelain art, would have made in this field! Nevertheless we can be thankful that this factory gave us a number of potpourri vases and brûle-parfums (Ill. 33). It is not until we arrive at the 20th century that we have a number of scent bottles worthy of attention (Ill. 277).

Naturally enough, Saxony's neighbouring ruler, Frederick II of Prussia, had to have his own manufacture. This did not come about until 1761, five years after the occupation of Meissen by his troops, when the Royal Factory was founded in Berlin with the help of Meissen ex-employees. Although they had the monarch's full support and possessed royal privileges they produced nothing that could measure up to Meissen standards. The bottle in Illustration 257, clearly modelled on a Meissen specimen (Ill. 192), is possibly of

Berlin manufacture. As far as our subject is concerned, only certain 19th century items are of interest. These would be bottles painted with the arms of the Prussian Court and views of royal residences. The two gift bottles (Ill. 270, 271) also have a certain charm. Egg shaped bottles seem to have been particularly popular in Berlin. Before the foundation of the Royal Manufacture in Berlin porcelain had already been made there: a Berlin merchant, Wilhelm Kaspar Wegely, started production in 1752 but his firm failed in 1756. An interesting specimen from his workshops is the bottle in Illustrations 205 and 206. It is typical of him that on this bottle where one would expect a depiction of Venus, we find, in fact, Mars.

South of the Alps the main manufactures are those of Capo di Monte, Le Nove and Doccia, from all of which flacons are known. A fine Capo di Monte bottle was illustrated in Kate Foster's book (1966, Plate 80) and is of particular interest since it shows on one side a portrait of Bonnie Prince Charlie (1720–1788) and on the other the coat of arms of the Countess of Bristol. It has the traditional oval shape. Entirely different and quite unusual but from the same factory is a series of figurine bottles, the dwarfs (court jesters?), hunchbacks and rogues depicted in humorous form (Ill. 228). The Doccia Factory near Florence was inspired by Vienna. Ware from this factory was not hard porcelain in the strictest sense. It is usually a light grey with a smeary glaze. Scent bottles are rare (Ill. 208, 209). Another Italian factory, Le Nove di Bassano, was founded by Antonibus Pasquale in 1752 with the help of the German porcelain painter, J. S. Fischer. It was more successful than Doccia in every respect. The only flacon known to have been made there is in Illustration 207.

18th century bottles show much less variation than those made in other countries and there are fewer of them. It is often difficult to determine the provenenace of those which have survived. One thing is sure: unlike all other factories, none of the French establishments copied the Meissen product. Scent bottles were made at Chantilly, Mennecy and Crepy-en-Valois. The very daring bottles in the form of a lady's leg come from Mennect. Some of these were also used as flea traps, particularly if there is decoration showing a group of fleas (Pulex irritans) on the shapely calf. A fine example in the Musée des Arts Décoratifs in Paris has a closure which indicates, however, use as a perfume container. Pot-pourri vases and brûle-parfums from French porcelain and faience factories are to be seen in almost every public collection. A real masterpiece is a pot-pourri vase in the form of a gondola. It has a greenish blue ground colour and is decorated with cupid scenes, was made in Sèvres and is attributed to Charles-Nicolas Dodin. Sèvres was the factory which was responsible for a vast quantity and variety of 19th century bottles, usually intended for toilet water.

One of the minor figures in scent bottle making was Emile Samson (1832–1913), whose creations often confront the curator and collector, as do, unfortunately, fakes. In 1845 he founded a firm in Paris under the name of his father, Edmé Samson (1810–1891) et Cie, which concentrated solely on reproduction pieces in porcelain, faience and enamel, the idea being to supply replacements for missing items in famous name dinner series and so on. Both Chinese porcelain and that of the great European factories including, of course, Meissen (Ill. 203) were imitated and eventually to such a degree of perfection that connoisseurs could be deceived. His Chelsea reproductions, however, are easy to identify since they were recreated in continental hard porcelain. He made reproductions, nota bene, not fakes, and this fact must be stated to do justice to the firm, which still exists. Unfortunately his mark is easily erased by those of dishonest intent, either by grinding it off or by using hydrofluoric acic; another category of cheats actually fake the reproductions using the "S" mark so that the question as to whether we have an original piece, a reproduction or a fake is very confused.

English factories

The "Girl in a Swing" factory and the Chelsea factory which followed

The first English porcelain was made in 1745, possibly slightly earlier. At any rate this date is mentioned in a memorandum from the Vincennes factory to Louis XV informing the monarch that England was producing porcelain more beautiful than Meissen.

The first factory was founded in Chelsea in the 18th century. As far as figures are concerned at least, the product here was not only totally different in style from English ceramics hitherto, but in its extravagant expression bordering on the frivolous also totally at variance with the sober taste of this insular people. The explanation is simple. Unlike most continental manufacturers the Chelsea factory was not founded under royal patronage, but was from the beginning a commercial undertaking without financial support from the purse of the ruler. With shrewd business sense, the entrepreneurs aimed at the export market and the Chelsea production was, therefore, in line with continental taste, that is the new rococo style. If we consider the scent bottle output alone we are soon aware that no other factory offered such a rich variety of tiny witty playthings. The economic explanation, however, is only half the story. As ever in her history, England, and especially its capital, was the haven for refugees from all countries. Space does not permit the consideration of the influence these immigrants, happily tolerated then quickly integrated, had on the intellectual, artistic and economic life of the nation throughout the centuries. Particular mention must, however, be made of the Huguenots who made their presence felt in this respect most notably in the 18th century. As far as porcelain is concerned, names of artists such as

François Roubiliac and Michael Rysbrak, and of the modeller Joseph Willems spring to mind. It does not, therefore, come as a surprise to learn that the Chelsea factory was the brainchild of a French jeweller, Charles Gouyn, and a Flemish silversmith, Nicholas Sprimont, originally from Liège. The earliest work from the new factory was naturally enough, considering the founder's crafts, influenced stylistically by metalwork and not by the wonders of Meissen. The first years of the partnership must have been stormy, for it was dissolved as early as 1749, and whereas Sprimont with private financial assistance carried on the Chelsea firm, which was later to be bought by William Duesbury of Derby, Gouyn founded a rival factory in Chelsea with the help of craftsmen from Staffordshire, or, according to other sources, men tempted from Sprimont's employ. This undertaking was short-lived and was at a standstill in the autumn of 1757 at the latest. Art historians, collectors and dealers have a difficult task in deciding whether pieces that have survived came from the period of the partnership or from the later separate efforts of the two partners. Much energy, time and ink has been devoted to this problem but no definite solutions arrived at. Some authors (Lane and Charleston, 1960 and K. Foster, 1966) bring further complications to our notice, suspecting, but without being able to produce documentary evidence, that one or indeed two other firms were also in competition. In view of the great quantity and prime importance of Chelsea scent bottles in collections and in the art market, we must take a brief look at their development. It must be noted that Chelsea bottles and related objects such as snuff boxes, patch boxes, watch fobs and so on were described at the time in trade and auction catalogues as "Chelsea porcelain toys", and still are (cf. p. 52).

One may assume with some certainty that during the brief partnership of Sprimont and Gouyn mainly tableware and not scent or smelling bottles was produced and that the original firm did not make such "toys" in the early years after Gouyn's departure.

Extensive research (Lane and Charleston) into a great many items, supported by chemical analysis, has shown that Gouyn was the original maker of these charming articles. His factory was known as the "Girl in a Swing Factory". The name is derived from a delightful porcelain figure, a girl on a swing suspended between two trees. This theme recurs throughout the rococo period – one only has to think of Fragonard's famous painting – and is met with in all its variations well into the 19th century. The original figure is in the Victoria and Albert Museum in London. As a jeweller, Gouyn knew what the market needed and, more importantly, he handled his material with all the experience of a goldsmith. His figures almost always have gold mounts and are notable for a certain elegance of form and superbly fine modelling. A characteristic figure has a slim body with a somewhat unnaturally small head on a long neck, particularly when the head serves as a stopper (Ill. 240) and this applies to animal figures also (Ill. 229). The porcelain mass of these figures, which are rarely more than 10 cm high, is light grey in colour. Decorative characteristics are the greyish-brown hair, sparse but subtly painted garden flowers and sometimes brown tinged leaves. Under the base one usually finds sprays of mixed garden flowers. All figures showing these features appear, on examination, to have been decorated by the same painter.

Among the most famous pieces are the following: 'Girl playing a lyre', "Pug Dog", "Parrot with Cochinchina Hen" (Ill. 229), "Billing doves" (Ill. 229), "Cupid as drummer boy" (Ill. 236), "Two Boys at a Still", and a flacon in the form of a bunch of flowers, the bound stems serving as toothpick or hairpin holders. Rarities are a rather untypical Chinese girl as a flacon and a very graceful swan scent bottle. Many pieces from the "Girl in a Swing" factory, including some scent bottles, have come down to us unpainted. The quantity of objects left in their white unpainted condition is surprisingly high: Lane and Charleston arrived at the sum of not fewer than 50 unpainted figures out of a total of 79 examined (1960). The reader who is familiar with the pressed glass inkwells which have stoppers in the form of busts of Voltaire or Goethe will not be surprised to find William Shakespeare as a scent bottle (Ill. 232, 233). This almost totally unpainted figure also emerged from the early factory and is based on a copy of the Shakespeare memorial in Poet's Corner, Westminster Abbey by Peter Scheemakers (after William Kent). This monument is no doubt the most reproduced one of the entire British Isles. Another rarity is to be found in the Victoria and Albert Museum: a 'Girl in a Swing' period porcelain box, with gold mount and painted with garden flowers, containing four glass bottles.

Deviating from the usual designs are a number of flacons which, although of high quality, do not fit in to the described pattern. The inferior gold mounts catch our attention along with the rather broken glazing, the chocolate brown eyes and hair, and the single rose motif under the base; the drapery is also usually only decorated with single roses. Some pieces have impressed mottos at the base. The violent turquoise of the leaf painting on and under the base is also noticeable. Whereas most experts attribute them to the "Girl in a Swing" factory, K. Foster (1966 and 1977) suspect that they came neither from this firm nor from the subsequent Chelsea factory, but have a third unknown source. Since it is hard to imagine that such an enterprise should have sunk without trace, it is perhaps safer to leave them for the moment under their old attribution. There is a possibility that the decoration of these pieces was done by outworkers, and that the painting was executed in some cases years after the manufacture of the figures. The most likely off-site painter in this respect was James Giles of Kentish Town (cf. Ill. 303, 305, 307), but William Duesbury could also have been involved. The modelling of all the figures is undoubtedly by one and the same hand.

The remaining scent bottles not already discussed are from the Chelsea factory carried on by Sprimont. On the basis of auction catalogues, newspaper advertisements and other evidence, attempts have been made to prove that the assets of the "Girl in a Swing" factory were bought up by Sprimont and that from 1754 Chelsea produced "toys", to satisfy the market. Even after the sale of the firm to William Duesbury in Derby in 1770 (the effects of the firm were not removed from Chelsea to Derby until 1784) scent bottles continued to be made. For those readers who enjoy art history detective work, the question arises as to why Sprimont did not use the moulds he is assumed to have inherited (a few bird moulds are assumed to have been used, but not with certainty). For the lover of these artefacts, however, such questions are of little import. Such a person will rather follow the dictum of a lady collector of the author's acquaintance: "Why should I worry where the kitchen is, when I am enjoying a good meal?" Nevertheless, it must be pointed out that the scent bottle production of the subsequent Chelsea factory may be divided into two periods.

The time from roughly 1755 to 1758 or slightly later is referred to as the 'red anchor' period, on account of the mark used during those years. A further confusion arises from the fact that Chelsea scent bottles, with one exception, bear no mark, unless we are in the presence of a fake. As if that were not enough, this applies to the "Girl in a Swing" flacons also.

Designs for bottles of the "red anchor" period are in the following categories: mainly animals, then scenes from fables, flowers such as tulips, and bouquets. In addition there is a series of monk and nun figures (Ill. 234). Yet again we meet with the monk smuggling the maiden of Meissen origin. Many of them have a bunch of flowers motif under the base and a gold serrated band around the lower edge of the base.

Finally, the bottles from the "gold anchor" period must be considered. Flacons from this period which began around 1758, even if in a few cases made from earlier moulds, are less clearly modelled but much more richly decorated and notable for the wealth of gold painting. The underside is usually green. Among the best known "gold anchor" pieces are "Orpheus playing on his lute", "Cupid with the Ass" (Ill. 230), "Goatherd with Billygoat", "The Fox and the Stork" from the fable of the same name, "Girl at the Spinning Wheel", and "Cupid in front of a rose bush". Particularly charming is the "Lover as Bird Catcher" (Ill. 242). A basket-like flacon with the inscription "Eau de Senteur" also slots into this group. Even after the removal to Derby (1784) scent bottles continued to be made. In the main they resemble those of the gold anchor period both stylistically and thematically, but are decorated in more glaring colours. The green underside of the case is often ringed in gold.

Only a few of the other English manufacturers made scent bottles in the 18th century and then on a very limited scale. Longton Hall, the first and shortlived Staffordshire factory founded by William Littler in 1750 certainly produced smelling bottles; a long necked bottle with an onion shaped body and blue underglaze painting in the Victoria and Albert Museum is evidence of this.

The Chelsea factory transferred to Derby manufactured scent bottles after 1784 under the aegis of William Duesbury. They were decorated with flower motifs and a blue diaper decoration and bore the signature SH.

The bottle in Figure 26 is of great interest. It comes from the Bristol factory which made soft porcelain and which flourished from 1749 to 1752 under the directorship of Benjamin Lund. The main ingredient of the porcelain here was steatit mined in Cornwall. The curious thing about this bottle is that its shape and facetted surface recall glass smelling bottles (Ill. 291) made half a century earlier, and that the same shape and technique occurs again roughly 25 years later in the well known cobalt blue scent bottles (Ill. 306). In its pleasing simplicity this beautiful smelling bottle provides a strong contrast with the extravagant Chelsea rococo bottles and heralds the transition to classical sobriety.

Opinions are divided, in matters of taste, on the subject of Wedgwood's jasper-ware (Ill. 227, 251, 252). It is everywhere: in Oxford Street's large department stores, at airport duty free shops and in the better shopping streets in the towns of Europe. You meet it in its blue and green garb *ad nauseam*. It is not the most original form of ornament for an English sitting room, but frequently has a place of honour there. If we are to understand its triumphal march through Europe in the 18th century, and why so many firms chose to imitate it, and to appreciate its quality at that time, we must wend our way to the major museums, putting the modern product out of our minds.

Josiah Wedgwood (1730–1795) was without doubt the most gifted English potter and the only one England produced who achieved international fame. His influence was felt throughout Europe, extending to Russia. After early efforts in Burslem in Staffordshire in 1754, efforts which were immediately crowned with success, he entered into a partnership in 1769 with Thomas Bentley (1730–1780), a businessman, and opened a larger factory with the name of Etruria, intending to manufacture decorative ceramics in the classical style. After years of experiments which cannot be gone into here, he developed the first jasper-ware upon which his international reputation was to be founded.

The extremely dense white material of waxy appearance was based on a formula the secret of which Wedgwood took with him to the grave. This

Fig. 26 Flacon in the form of a pilgrim's flask. Porcelain with shallow facets and decorated with coloured flowers and birds on a white ground. Unmounted. England, Bristol (Benjamin Lund), c. 1750. H. 75 mm. Drawn from a piece in the BM.

would explain why after his demise the same quality was never again attained. The white moulded reliefs typical of this ware were very carefully pressed into the surface of the vessel and hand finished by a skilled craftsman after the final firing process was accomplished. In early pieces the basic material is always coloured with oxidising materials; in later ones the white ware was either dipped in a coloured mixture, or the latter was applied by brush. The second cheaper method proved to be the better one.

There is not absolute consistency in colour, blue or green, owing to the marginal differences in the cobalt quantities added to the mixture and to temperature variations in the kiln, but therein lies the charm of the pieces made in the 1770's in contrast with the monotony of tone in later ones. Although most jasper-ware has a blue fond, shades of green were obtained by using iron as well as cobalt: sea green, mignonette green and, very rare and therefore much sought after, olive green. Black jasper-ware was also made and a little yellow. Particularly rare are pieces with a white fond and blue reliefs.

Design for the reliefs was entrusted to artists of repute such as John Flaxman, George Stubbs, Lady Templeton and James Tassie. The motifs on scent bottles are mainly inspired by Greek and Roman mythology, but there are also relief portraits as found on the countless Wedgwood medallions. Although idealised, these portraits of famous people of the day are, nevertheless, reasonably accurate and, therefore, an important historical source.

The small size of Wedgwood scent bottles is the reason for their lack of mark or signature. It is, therefore, often difficult, if not impossible, to distinguish genuine pieces from good imitations by competitors such as Turner and Neal (Ill. 253). 19th century German and American reproductions are easy to recognise since the basis and the relief decoration were not executed separately but formed as a whole, so that we often have a negative imprint on the inside of the vessel.

At least as far as smelling bottles are concerned, jasper-ware represents the last high point of ceramic art in England. After a period which saw England's porcelain output dominated by the extravagant rococo style favoured on the Continent, it was Wedgwood, rather than the many other artists of his time, who, with his restrained and noble forms and his admiration for the designs of classical antiquity, influenced and gave direction to contemporary taste.

19th century English scent bottles

Only three firms among those who made scent bottles in the 19th century are worthy of note. The world famous firm of Spode founded in 1733 in Stoke on Trent (merged with W. T. Copeland since 1813) is one of these, and a signed bottle from this factory was in the author's possession until he regrettably gave it away and heard of it no more. Attractive bottles, but hard to find, are those made by the firm of Coalport in Shropshire. This factory was founded in 1796 by John Rose and is still in operation, nowadays, however, in Stoke on Trent. In the 19th century it was famous for its Sèvres and Meissen imitations, but in the second half developed a pretty flower-decorated ware with coloured fond. Bottles of this period appear in the trade from time to time. The British firm with the longest history of manufacture and of being on the same site is the Worcester Royal Porcelain Factory founded in 1751. Within a year of its foundation it took over the Bristol firm of Lund already mentioned and thereby inherited its production secrets. The technique of transfer printing was first used in Worcester, indeed as early as 1755. An historical curiosity is the fact that shortly afterwards the transfer print portrait of Frederick II of Prussia appeared on all sorts of items being made at the factory. What was the reason for this? The "protestant hero" had marched into Dresden in 1756 and helpfully destroyed England's main rival in the field of porcelain making. In English eyes he was really "the Great".

In connection with perfume, as far as we can tell, only pot-pourri vases and pastille burners were made at Worcester until the mid 19th century. Not until 1845 did they turn their attention to scent bottles but from then until the turn of the century they produced far more of these items than all the other English factories put together. Although mass produced, the bottles have a certain charm and grace the display cabinets of many serious collectors. At the second World Exhibition held in London in 1862, Worcester exhibited its ivory porcelain for the first time. Many bottles were made in this material, which resembles real ivory closely in tone, and were painted with motifs from nature. To reinforce the ivory connection, copies of genuine ivory carvings were made in this porcelain. The flacon in Fig. 1 is very rare and would seem to be an impractical container, until one realises that there is an inner lining. Items with pierced surfaces were made at many European factories, beginning with a vase in Böttger porcelain at Meissen. The technique undoubtedly reached its zenith at the Worcester Royal Porcelain Factory. The master of the art was George Owen, who created pieces in the last quarter of the 19th century and later which border on the miraculous, so fine is the pierced workmanship. They are no doubt inspired by the intricacies of oriental ivory carving, hence the need for an ivory coloured porcelain which was given a thin covering of pink. Chinese vessels from the Ming dynasty were perhaps another source of inspiration. Imitations of this ware were made by the firm of Thomas Grainger (founded in Worcester in 1801 and later absorbed into the Worcester Royal Porcelain Factory) but instead of being individually crafted, they were obtained by the use of templates. Five bottles known to be by Owen are in the Dyson Perrins Museum in Worcester. Another rare category are the Worcester bottles decorated by Palmere after Teniers and Watteau. Queen Victoria's golden jubilee in 1887 gave an impetus to the souvenir industry and this is also reflected in the production.

One would not have expected the answer "a birds egg", if one had asked a Victorian lady what she carried in her purse, that is, unless one understood that this was a man-made useful accessory, indeed a scent bottle, as those who have had one handed down as one of great grandmama's little treasures will be aware. As early as 1836 a Sunderland firm was making gift eggs, that is, scent bottles in the form of eggs, but the firm ceased to exist, and it was not until 1865 that the idea was taken up again by James Macintyre in his 'Washington China Works'. He is responsible for a vast quantity of flacons, all exact copies of eggs from birds in the native avifauna (Ill. 269). The smallest is the robin egg bottle and the largest the swan egg. They were registered at the Patent Office in London on the 29th January 1885 under the number 28772 as "porcelain bird's eggs scent bottles". They all have a silver mount and usually have a screw closure in the form of a bird's head. Similar egg scent bottles were made in glass at the same period in England, but by whom is not known.

The rapid expansion of the railways in Europe in the second half of the 19th century and the simultaneous increase in the wealth of the middle classes meant a more mobile population. Year by year thousands and thousands of people streamed into the seaside resorts, which did not merely offer an opportunity for sea bathing but provided entertainments to suit every taste. At the end of the stay, the 19th century tourist naturally enough wanted to show where he had been and acquire some tangible souvenir to take home with him. This period saw the invention of the picture postcard and the rise of the souvenir industry which was soon providing a living for a huge workforce. Were one rich enough, what could be more amusing than to start a collection of curiosities from one's travels? The Eiffel Tower made of soap, the yawning leather crocodile with his inscription "Bad Schlagenbad" and the childish nymph in Illustration 274. There were yet further possibilities and if one had the patience one could collect scent bottles with views or arms of almost every European town of note. There were even flacons bearing portraits of people, famous and infamous. One might carry home a memento of Richard Wagner, or one of the many representations of Lily Langtry, acress and mistress of Edward VII, or of Marie Antoinette (Ill. 272) or of an unidentified figure from the Mikado.

So much for the taste of the petty bourgeois in Victorian England. Looking for a mark on the base of the child nymph flacon we find in large letters the word GERMANY and when we examine other objects, not necessarily scent bottles, we see "Made in Bavaria", and, as investigation has shown, other souvenirs, in spite of their English mounts, were made by the firm of P. Donath in Silesia.

Of all materials used for making containers, glass is the only one which allows the contents to be seen. Glass, by definition not a solid with a fixed crystal structure, but an undercooled liquid, is suitable on account of its very quality of transparency, particularly if those liquids are of an attractive colour. What could be more delightful to the eye than a carafe of burgundy against the sunlight, or a row of glass bottles full of costly perfumes ranging in colour from pale sea green to deep amber? Glass, then, can be subservient to its contents and it is only by design and decorative treatment of its surface that it comes to the fore, not merely complementing what it holds but a thing of beauty in itself.

For the lover or fine glass the present century's return to the notion of its purity after various erroneous treatments of the material and ventures down many an artistic cul-de-sac, is very gratifying. A glance round the cosmetic departments of large department stores shows that the modern perfume industry favours glass almost exclusively for the vast array of containers for its products. Throughout perfume history there has never been such a plethora of scent bottles of every design.

This preference for glass has not come about solely for aesthetic reasons, of course, for glass containers are considerably cheaper to produce than those in other materials. In addition glass in its molten state can be formed into an endless variety of shapes which could only be obtained, if at all, by more complicated and expensive techniques in other materials. It is also eminently suited to automated mass production methods. Even so, ideal it is not, and the reason for this lies in the deteriotation of perfume when exposed to light. The real connoisseur of perfumes will expose them as little as possible to it. Leaving aside, however, the immense number of modern scent bottles, for which there is not space in a book dedicated mainly to those of past centuries, it is clear that the majority of the latter were, in fact, also made of glass.

Many glass items, and this applies to glass of the ancient world, had colour tinges of varying intensity as a result of the presence of heavy metal salts (copper, cobalt, iron etc.). Iron salts in the sands used in the making gave the glass produced in continental glass houses a greenish, bluish green or often brown colouring. Glass showing this impurity was known in Germany as "Waldglas". This is of interest, because medical bottles of the 16th and 17th centuries were in this type of glass, and it is from these that scent bottles, and among them the well known "Rosolenflaschen" for Eau de Cologne are descended (Fig. 22; Ill. 289).

The glassmaker's dream came true in Venice in the 16th century when it was discovered how to make a glass so clear and pure that it resembled rock crystal but was obtained at a fraction of the cost. The secret was the addition of manganese and certain other chemicals. It is not surprising that the rock crystal-like metal was treated by glasshouses north of the Alps in the manner of rock crystal itself, i. e. via the technique used for semi-precious stones

(Ill. 297). It is ironic that after this great and epoch making contribution to glass technology made by the Venetians later generations in every country put much effort, expense and ingenuity into investigating methods of colouring glass. Sometimes the entire glass mass was coloured, sometimes it had coloured inclusions or had a coloured surface layer. In the first category the discovery of ruby glass, often attributed to Johann Kunckel, was one of the major German contributions in glass history (Ill. 283, 331). By the admixture of cobalt complexes and copper salts, blue and green glasses of fine quality were produced, particularly in England (Ill. 281, 282). There is a tendency in England to refer to all fine pieces of cobalt blue glass as "Bristol", but this is erroneous and it has been known for some time that they were made in South Staffordshire glasshouses. The term "Bristol Glass" must, therefore, be viewed as an antique trade term rather than an historical truth. This also applies, mutatis mutandis, to the term Nailsea. When considering coloured glass we must not omit the so-called milk glass which was wide-spread in Germany and Bohemia and which reached its greatest perfection in England (Ill. 304, 305). In spite of the many fine milk glass scent bottles and other vessels, this type of glass represents a denial of the character of glass and must be seen as an artistic deviation; in their extreme form some bottles cannot be distinguished from their porcelain counterparts (a comparison between Ill. 204 and 205 clearly demonstrates this point). Coloured glass was, however, the ideal material in which to make smelling bottles, hiding ugly corroded inner walls from view.

Almost all processes of glass technology had been known since Roman times, as, for example, the manufacture of millefiori glass (Ill. 349) and overlay glass (Ill. 352, 353). An innovation came in the 16th century with the Venetian Latticinoglass (Italian latte = milk) or "vetro a reticelli" later known as "Netzglaser" (German Netz = net). There is hardly any shape or type of decoration suitable for glass which is not found when we consider scent bottles; the illustrations speak for themselves.

Unlike objects in metal which have a mark, or in porcelain which often have at least an indication of the factory of origin, glass scent bottles, provide us with no means of identifying the craftsmen responsible for their making. If one excludes many of the superb German flacons from the late 17th and early 18th centuries (e. g. Ill. 283) one may state without reservation that English scent bottles of the second half of the eighteenth century are among the noblest creations in glass in the history of perfume. The reasons are not hard to find: the glass quality (lead glass was used), harmony of form, the excellence of the cutting and last but not least the first class painted decoration (Ill. 281, 300, 303–307). A considerable contribution to the beautification of these small delights was made by James Giles (1718–1780), working in Soho, also well known as a porcelain painter. From his hand, no doubt with the assistance of apprentices, came the decorations which were so ingeniously superimposed on the curvatures of the flacons and their facet cutting (Ill. 303, 305, 307).

Flacons which combine glass and porcelain, representing a technical innovation, allow us to trace their place of origin, and quite often the actual maker. These are the bottles which enclose within the glass mass a portrait, usually white, made of fired ceramic paste (Ill. 311, 312). This techniqe was developed in late 18th century France; its principal exponents there were Josquin Desprez and Pierre Honoré Boudon de Saint-Amans. In England the most famous glassmaker of his day, Apsley Pellatt, had his method for the manufacture of this "crystallo ceramie" patented. He produced hundreds of small objects in glass, among them many scent bottles (Ill. 312) of outstanding quality and beauty. German, Austrian and Bohemian glasshouses took over the technique and made bottles which could hold their own with both the French and English product.

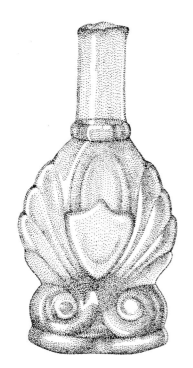

Fig. 27   Mass produced throwaway flacon, mainly used for lavender water and sold together with lavender-scented soap. Sea-green glass, mechanical blown. Found on a refuse tip. England, c. 1880–1885. P. London

Reference was made in the chapter on porcelain to the boom in scent bottle production in the 19th century, particularly during the second half (Fig. 27). To gain an impression of the quantity of flacons from the Biedermeier period alone, one only has to visit the Kunstgewerbemuseum in Prague or the relevant museums in Vienna. The pattern books of Bohemian, French and English glasshouses show a wealth of bottles in every imaginable shape and style and which range from the practical and beautiful to the scurrilous and tasteless (Ill. 313, 333, 336). Walter Spiegel (1984) has devoted a comprehensive study, practically a monograph, to the bottles of this period which makes worthwhile reading. Most worthy of note are the bottles which the skilled glass cutter has succeeded in turning into small jewels. It is not always easy, indeed often impossible, to decide whether these bottles are of English or Bohemian origin. The matter is further complicated by the fact that numerous Bohemian and German glass cutters worked in English glass houses in the second half of the 19th century.

Most of these bottles are in clear glass and sometimes lightly coloured, but setting aside this largest category, the impression we have when viewing a large collection of glass from the Biedermeier period and the following decades of the 19th century is that all the colours of the rainbow are before us. The disguising of the very nature of glass through all kinds of colouring techniques was most widely practised in this period. Hyalith and lithyalin glass, milk glass with coloured overlay, agate and opaline glass, agate and amber glass, to name only the most important, are richly represented by flacons from Bohemian glass houses, especially those by Friedrich Egermann and Buquoy (Ill. 31, 285).

Bottles made in two or more layers of cased glass and cut artistically with great precision were brought on to the market in their thousands by Bohemian, German and particularly English glass houses (Ill. 333, 336, 343, 352). Never before in the history of perfume was there such a weird and wonderful selection of containers. No wonder that the new century looked for something less elaborate in form and embellishment.

Double flacons

In the second half of the 19th century scent bottles and smelling bottles were essential accessories for every lady. The vinaigrette was outmoded and hardly used. It is easy to understand how necessary it was to have recourse to smelling salts when one thinks of heavy late Victorian interiors, badly ventilated, dripping with pompons and plush, and when one realises that writing paper, book marks, bed linen, the linings of jewel boxes, and, most particularly, handkerchiefs were all perfumed; heliotrope, sandalwood, musk, lavender, and other scents pervaded the whole ambiance and masked bad odours. The combining of the two types of container mentioned above was inevitable, but we do not know who first made a double bottle to fill this gap in the market. The double bottle per se was not new; as early as the 17th century one finds bottles fused side by side. They were often bladder shaped and used for oil and vinegar or other domestic necessities or for pharmaceutical preparations. Now and again they have a common foot so that they can stand on the table. These bottles, also known as "gimmel flasks" had both openings together at the same end.

The original idea of fusing the two bottles end to end with openings at each extremity was a mid century English invention. The oldest one known dates from 1851 (Birmingham). The success must have been phenomenal as evidenced by the quantity of such bottles found in the antique trade. No handbag or muff could have been without one. With a few exceptions, they were not particularly elegant pieces, and one asks oneself whether the modern woman would be prepared to carry around bottles of this weight and size.

Double scent bottles were sold into the 20th century but had their heyday between 1865 and 1890. In spite of their basic form and common features these bottles show an immense variety hardly met with in any other category. The materials used were metal (usually silver) or gilded alloys, very occasionally porcelain, but usually glass (Ill. 345–348). In its basic form the double bottle is the plain or angular cylinder. Both compartments are usually of the same length, were generally made separately and then fused together. In best quality bottles the joint is almost invisible. Although most were cheaper mass produced items with pewter or brass lids, one comes across more individual and costly examples (Ill. 348).

Most are in coloured glass, the reason being the same as those in the case of the smelling bottle. Red, blue and green are the commonest colours; rarer are bottles in "annagrün" and "annagelb" (these are glasses with a luminous green or yellow colour which is due to the addition of small quantities of uranium. It was mainly manufactured by Joseph Riedel of Polaun and first traded around 1850. He named these radiant glasses after his wife Anna); there are a few in milk glass. Rare and rather ugly are double bottles with the two compartments in different colours, and those in cased glass are uncommon. The perfume compartment is usually sealed by means of a metal cap under which, in better pieces, there is a glass stopper. The smelling salts compartment in cheaper bottles is closed by screw lid with cork seal or with a well fitting glass stopper and screw or hinge lid. Better quality pieces will have the patent closure as described for smelling bottles (p. 30). The caps may be plain or richly engraved or repoussé, in some cases having a blank area for the owner's monogram. Some are further embellished with a "precious stone" made of glass, a semi-precious stone or a coral pearl. Expensive double bottles were often sold, as were smelling bottles, in their own leather case (Ill. 347, 348), the satin lining of which was often stamped with the firm's name.

The double bottle went through all kinds of changes in the course of time, not only in form, but in function, and is at times highly original, as for example in the combination of bottle and whistle or the imitation opera glasses (Ill. 346). In the latter case the centre metal mount contains either a vinaigrette, a box or a flat hollow intended to hold a photograph. There was no limit to the fantasy of these creations. An example owned by the pianist Ignaz Moschele is in the form of a cross, that is, with four compartments. If the vinaigrette was combined with a scent bottle, there was a problem of discrepancy of size. There were various attempts to solve this, among them the double scent bottle in the form of a hunting horn must have been quite popular (Ill. 299, 319). The short chain usually attached to this type of bottle indicates that it was worn at the belt. The silver mounts on double scent bottles almost exclusively show the London (the lion head) and Birmingham (the anchor) discharge marks. The fact that there is frequently no mark is no indication that the mount is not English. The silver content of the metal on these mass-produced bottles was often so slight that it did not conform to assay standards. Good quality mounts always bear the "Assay Office" mark and year code and almost always have a craftsman's or manufacturer's mark.

Lalique

René Lalique (1860–1945) came from Ay in Champagne, and the life and landscape of that region was later reflected in his art. He studied in Paris at the Ecole des Arts Décoratifs and for two years at a London art school. In his early career he worked as a silversmith and jewellery designer for his teacher, Louis Ancoc. In 1885 he opened his first workshop in the Place Gaillon and in 1890 his first jewellery shop in the Place Vendôme. His exclusive creations were exhibited in the elegant shops in the Rue de la Paix, and they were worn by Sarah Bernhardt and other stars of the Paris firmament, not forgetting Madame la Présidente herself. His jewellery with its fused colours and paste stones, often in the form of butterflies, dragonflies and other creatures in the taste of the late Art Nouveau period brought him fame in the nineties in France and indeed the whole of Europe. At the turn of the century, especially after the World Exhibition in Paris in 1900, he was counted among the small number of great jewellers of the world.

It was probably his efforts to discover means of making artificial gems which led to his turning his hand to glass making. His first attempts in this field were shaped vessels in the cire perdue technique (lost wax technique) and as a result each piece was individual. His first glass house where he made lamps, vases, bowls etc., was situated near Paris and it was here too that he embarked on scent bottle design.

The contract came from François Coty, probably in 1906, with the instructions: "Offer a woman the best product you can make and present it in a perfect container (beautiful, simple, but in the best possible taste), ask a reasonable price for it, and you will have a commercial proposition such as the world has never seen." Truly a tremendous goal and it was attained to the desired artistic and business standards. This was only made possible by means of series production, that is the manufacture of large quantities of small artistic items without sinking to the level of mass ware. Every flacon that came from Lalique's glass house was singularly elegant and exuded luxury (Ill. 363–368). Even a non-collector, even the most ardent disposer of the non-essential, would have found it hard to throw an empty Lalique bottle into the dustbin. It is probably thanks to his scent bottles that the name of Lalique is known so widely today.

The earliest bottles designed for Coty did not come from Lalique's own glass house, but were made by Legras & Cie in St. Denis. It was only after he had opened his second glass house in Combs-la-Ville, east of Paris – around or shortly after 1909 – and after he had (completely) gone over to glassmaking that he started to manufacture flacons for Coty and other perfume manufacturers such as Houbigant, Nina Ricci, Worth, Roger et Gallet and Forvil. His early works, especially the scent bottles, are still strongly influenced by the Art Nouveau style yet the motifs tend to be of a timeless classical nature. In contrast with other glass artists of the Art Nouveau period who gained their best effects through the use of colour, Lalique reverted to an awareness of the purity of clear glass. He used it not merely as a vehicle for decorative effects, but exploited its transparency, its shine and its quality of reflection to express his artistic vision and to create bottles which were at the same time useful and practical. He seldom used colours and when he did it was to give the entire object a film of pastel colour; a soft pink, blue or metallic blue-green were the preferred colours; occasionally amber coloured glass is found.

The power of refraction was increased by cutting in relief, and the alternate matt and polished areas of the bottles produced a satisfying contrasting effect. In his glass pieces with relief work the main decorative elements stand out from a matt background. The reliefs were made by sandblasting or acid etching techniques. The influence of the Bauhaus movement is evident in the architectural effect of certain flacons and perfume burners (Ill. 32).

Among his most exciting creations are bottles such as "Bouchon fleurs de Pommiers", "Lunaria", "Telline", and "Perles" (Ill. 367).

"Lunaria" is an onion shaped bottle in clear glass, decorated with flat green fruits (siliculae) of the attractive plant honesty (Lunaria annua). The botanist will notice with satisfaction, and this speaks well for Lalique's powers of observation, the exact number and correct position of the organs of the flower which serves as a stopper. A rare piece is "Hirondelles", an almost square bottle the entire surface of which has a satin matt finish forming the background to a flock of swallows in relief. It is unfortunately not possible to state with certainty whether this bottle, or indeed most others, was made for a particular perfume. Even if a flacon were found in its original packaging, one could not say that it was intended solely for the named perfume, since several of the Coty perfumes, such as Muguet, Violette and Chypre were on the market for years and since Coty used each of the bottles he commissioned for various perfumes. This was possibly the practice of other manufacturers also.

One cannot speak of Lalique without mentioning his veneration of the female form in the motifs of a series of his flacons and perfume sprays. Swathed in diaphanous veils, these goddesses of the dance are among the finest creations in glass for erotic effect. Totally lacking in vulgarity they reflect the spirit of the Belle Epoque and the elegance of the most civilised metropolis of the world. Lalique was inspired by, among many other artistes, the greatest dancers of his day, Loie Fuller and Isadora Duncan. The first of these two Americans would perform in diaphanous veils on a brightly lit stage or indeed on a glass floor illuminated from below, and the second was known for her barefoot interpretation of Greek style dancing (Ill. 287, 368).

A number of his designs for flacons were executed in different sizes; thus his dressing table sets will usually include, along with the dishes and powder bowls, four bottles of different size. The "Perles" design already mentioned (Ill. 367) occurs in other versions, not unusually in frosted glass with blue enamel decoration. The "Dahlia" set, still produced today, was made in several variations, namely white, peach coloured or greenish, usually matt and with black anthers.

Lalique's liking for motifs from the plant kingdom is evident from his scent bottles (Ill. 363, 364, 366). His "Fleurs concaves" is an upright thick-walled clear glass bottle with brown stylised flowers fused into the body. A

rare piece is 'Cyclamen', a masterpiece made for Coty. The cyclamen is, however, most unobtrusive: the sides of the narrow vase-like hexagonal bottle has a flower on the upper part below which nymphs form the main decorative element, their finely veined dragonfly wings reaching elegantly down to the base of the piece.

Up to now only scent bottles which undoubtedly represent the finest aspect of Lalique's work of this kind have been mentioned, but he was also responsible for countless small more common bottles which are nevertheless worth considering and of which no collector need be ashamed even though they can only be described as mass produced.

To this category belongs the bottle made for Worth's "Imprudence", with its superimposed ring design giving it the look of a high voltage insulator. Another well known bottle is square decorated with a glass rope tied into a knot. Nor must we overlook the many attractive little bottles with very elegant albeit impractical stoppers in the form of birds and sea creatures.

As far as Lalique's position in the history of art history is concerned, art and glass historians are of divided opinion. Not everyone would agree with Calouste Fulbenkian who called his friend one of the greatest men in the history of art; his genius is, however, beyond question and his service to the French perfume industry immeasurable. This would account for the many imitations of his art, although they are never quite convincing (Fig. 30, 31;

Fig. 28   Toilet set comprising a lidded powder box, flacon and atomiser. Black, partly silvered pressed glass. Czechoslovakia, 1920's. H. 185 mm (flacon), 70 mm (atomiser), 65 mm (box). C. Schwarzkopf

Fig. 29   Atomiser for cologne. Cut crystal glass with patented chromium mount. France, Baccarat, Marcel, Franck, 1920's. H. 110 mm. C. Schwarzkopf

Fig. 30 Flacon. Mould-blown opaque glass with matt surface. France, Paris (Etling), 1920's. H. 160 mm. C. Schwarzkopf

Fig. 31 Flacons and an atomiser, from a toilet set of six pieces. Colourless pressed glass with matt surfaces. Decorated, in relief, with elephants' heads holding bouquets in their trunks. Atomiser with brass mount and red rubber bulb. France, 1920's. H. (f. r. to l.) 165 mm, 135 mm, 130 mm. C. Schwarzkopf

Ill. 327). Lalique's firm is carried on by his son at the present time. Since Lalique's death the letter R has been discontinued as part of his signature on the firms products. It is a pity that so many of the old designs are still produced, the result being that one simply sees them too often.

Marinot

Containers for perfume are, like all objects in the applied arts, primarily functional. It seems, therefore, paradoxical to devote space to the work of a man who conceived vessels with such names as vase, beaker, bottle and flacon as pure works of art, without giving any consideration to their practical use. Every piece of glass designed by Maurice Marinot is as unique as the man himself in the history of glass making. This would explain the limited number of works he produced: Marinot glasses are among the great rarities of the art market and museums are not exactly flooded with them. Whatever the artist's intention may have been no one will offend his creations (Ill. 358–360) by actually using them as scent bottles. As a matter of fact a fine perfume will enhance the beauty of his flacons as a deep red port wine would his larger vessels.

It is a curious fact that the three most important glass artists of the late 19th and early 20th century, Gallé (Fig. 32; Ill. 361, 362), Lalique and Marinot were all sons of a country whose achievements in glassmaking down the centuries had been poor compared with those of other lands.

Like Lalique, Marinot, a painter from Troyes, came to glassmaking late in life, after visiting the glass house of Viard in Bar-sur-Seine in the year 1911. A mere three years later a critic was writing "In Maurice Marinot's work we see a return to pure glass, to light transparent glass, decorated, however, with enamel in cheerful blue and red, always exciting in its effect". The enamel decoration referred to consists of restrained figurative decoration on some of his bottles, a characteristic example being on display in the Victoria and Albert Museum, in a collection of not fewer than twenty Marinot pieces.

In his later work colour is of minor importance and his feeling for the material, his effective exploitation of its brightness and transparency, finds its supreme expression. Whereas one notes architectural elements in Lalique's pieces, in Marinot's it is the influence of sculpture with its flowing lines which is evident. One of the earliest examples of his command of his art is the bottle in Illustration 358. Proof that Marinot creations were not products of chance is in the many preparatory sketches he left behind. His competent use of the acid bath technique may astound us, but the way he incorporated air bubbles, usually considered a defect, into his designs shows an amazing degree of technical and artistic ability never equalled before or after him. One is bound to ask how it was technically possible to control the air bubbles in such a way that they were evenly distributed in the inner wall of the bottle (Ill. 359) or that they took upon themselves a pattern of effervescent champagne (Ill. 358) reaching their highest concentration in the stopper, which was made separately.

Fig. 32 Flacon. So-called "Clare de Lune glass". Colourless glass painted with delicate enamel colours. France, 1880, signed E. Gallé. Collection G. Gros

The elaborate accessories required by the well dressed person in the 18th century included the chatelaine which is of interest to us only in that some examples had an attached scent bottle. The word chatelaine means "guardian of the castle", that is the keeper of the keys. The history of the object in question goes back to the middle ages. It consisted of a jointed metal belt to which were attached keys and other items of practical use, which in the convent would mean breviary and crucifix as well. It was usually worn around the waist.

In the course of time it increasingly took on the character of an ornament, and splendid examples were made in the 18th century. It was worn by both sexes and was in gold, silver, and later also in tombak (a copper-zinc alloy). The principal attachments were artistically made etuis or a valuable watch; in addition on little golden chains there might be all kinds of small attachments such as watchkeys, small seals, amulets, a writing tablet pencil, thimble and

CHATELAINES, ETUIS, TOILET BOXES AND NECESSAIRES

small charms in metal, ivory, porcelain and so on. A scent bottle, or even several of them, would not infrequently be included, if not hanging directly from the belt, then in etuis or in small boxes on each side (Ill. 330). If worn by gentlemen, the chatelaine was usually longer and hung with more attachments.

In France, the chatelaine, like so many other extravagant playthings of the aristocracy, was a victim of the Revolution, and in the rest of Europe its manufacture died a natural death at the turn of the century. Only in England and Germany was the tradition continued, their anachronistic creations being in the former country often in cut steel and in the latter in Berlin ironwork.

A considerably simpler form of chatelaine consisted of a chain suspended between two buttons, pins or pegs and was worn exclusively by ladies but not necessarily at the waist. Scent bottles were often attached to it. In common with many other types of ornament, the chatelaine enjoyed a revival during the "second rococo", especially in Victorian England; it was not, however, intended for the aristocracy but for the middle classes surging upward on a wave of prosperity. Firms in London and Birmingham made chatelaines in base metals, usually brass, occasionally in tombak and sometimes in silver. The firms of Drew in Leadenhall Street and Liberty sold chatelaines in the "Dutch and Flemish styles". The etui was the central feature of a chatelaine, but it also had a separate existence and was either to be found on the dressing table or in a lady's purse. Gentlemen may have carried one in their coat pocket.

In the 17th and 18th centuries it was a cylindrical or square object, longish, narrowing to its base and usually richly decorated. It contained articles such as scissors, penknives, tweezers, ear spoons, pencils, writing tablets and sometimes a small scent bottle.

In the 18th and in the course of the 19th century precious metals were replaced by other materials and the term etui used for containers which only held a group of specific objects such as, for example, two or three scent bottles (Ill. 332). Eventually there were etuis made for one object only (Ill. 347, 348).

Valuable bottles had been sold since the 17th century in etuis specially made for them. These etuis were simple and undecorated in wood, leather or papier mâché and either lacquered or covered in thin leather or fish skin (Ill. 100, 125, 150, 208, 291, 348). We know that Chelsea bottles were sold in such etuis.

The protection of the etui was necessary for gilded bottles or those with applied gemstones to prevent surface wear or loss of the stones as happened if the bottles were carried loose.

A more elegant version and designed as an object of beauty in its own right was the 19th century development of the etui, which was intended for one or more bottles and made of ivory, mother of pearl, tortoiseshell, bone or even celluloid. The monogram of the owner is often to be found on the lid.

When intended for the dressing table the etui was more often in the form of a casket. There is a degree of overlapping in design and function in the matter of all these containers, so the terms etuis, box and casket are difficult to define.

Toilet boxes or caskets, the craftsman's imagination knew no bounds in their design: they came in every guise. The Wellcome Collection in London has, for example, one in the form of a cradle, if such a fanciful item may still be termed a casket.

Less unusual, but often richly decorated and made in costly materials are the perfume or toilet boxes which contain scent bottles along with other items. In the latter case they form a link with the necessaire to be discussed later. In their simplest form they are wooden boxes with neat compartments holding a range of equipment consisting of two or more scent bottles, a metal funnel and not infrequently a mixing dish (Ill. 331). Such perfume sets enabled the owner to mix his or her own fragrances. This practice is hard for us to imagine today, used as we are to pre-blended, pre-packed designer perfumes. Since these sets were also taken on journeys, the compartments and lid of the container were upholstered in silk or velvet. A much more elaborate version is the cupboard set, complete with drawers and hinged doors. Such toilet cupboards are often exhibited in museums as domestic medicine chests; in many cases they serve this as well as a cosmetic purpose.

From the 17th century onwards perfume boxes were often disguised as books, particularly in Italy. These flat containers, rather like cigar boxes, were "bound" in leather and often fitted with a decorative book clasp. The inside was divided into compartments and lined with cotton wool. Each compartment contained a glass phial in which was some perfume essence or other. The inner side of the hinged lid contained a hand-coloured print or a decorative trade paper.

If asked what was the most typical, most popular and most used item of the 18th century one could safely say that it was the necessaire, the only qualification being that it was restricted to the upper classes who also were the fashion leaders – as far as France is concerned at least until the outbreak of revolution in 1789.

Along with the mirror it was the item which was absolutely essential for the toilette at a time when ladies and gentlemen devoted hours of their time to the business of dressing, undressing and changing their costumes. These vanity boxes contained everything one needed in the way of cosmetics, or for the coiffure, the pedicure and so on. They might contain writing materials and not infrequently a coffee service and cutlery, but such impedimenta take us beyond the scope of this book. The necessaire would stand on the dressing table or be taken on journeys or hunting expeditions. Its size and design would be such that it was suitable for both undertakings. Some very beautiful necessaires of modest dimensions were also produced in England from 1770 onwards. They were often small agate boxes decorated with fine gold mounts. They contained from two to six flacons of the same type.

Later in the early 19th century, finely cut or engraved glass bottles were made for the toilet waters and perfumes of the necessaire (Ill. 322, 329). A particularly attractive collection of such necessaires is to be seen in the Brighton Museum. In its more sober form Ill. 354 shows us a later example from the Germany of the "Gründerzeit" (a period stretching from the victorious end of the Franco-Prussian war to the turn of the century).

PERFUMED POWDER   Powder, with other forms of makeup, is essential ammunition in the armoury of vanity. Its practical use in medical and child care does not concern us here. Powder has been used for centuries in an attempt to hide the effects of ageing. It was an aid to self deception. The betrayal of white hair was obviated by the general use of powder by both sexes, in a powder crazy age, on the coiffure, be it natural or a wig; even children were not spared. In daily hygiene powder was a substitute for washing and the ritual of powdering occupied a good portion of the day. Since even when abroad, the immaculately powdered effect had to be maintained, the powder box and powder brush (often a hare's foot) were not missing from the travelling chest. Various ingenious methods of accomplishing even powdering were devised (Ill. 171).

A peep into the cosmetic section of any department store will reveal that the use of powder has by no means died out. When it began is diffucult to say. Evelyn writes that "painting and similar tricks of the toilet did not become established among respectable women before the spring of 1654". And for less respectable women?

As far as our theme is concerned, powder and makeup are of interest only inasmuch as they contain perfumed elements. An ancestor of modern make-up preparations was the widely used 19th century "Pomade Divine". It was composed of orris-root powder, cinnamon, cloves, nutmeg, storax, camphor, rose oil, benzoin and lard. An interesting fact is that modern medicine makes use of benzoic acid for the treatment of eczema and dermatitis. The ladies and gentlemen of the 19th century were, therefore, unconsciously, to use a possibly inappropriate metaphor, killing two birds with one stone.

Among the perfumed powders created for cosmetic use, Yardley's Lavender powder is of worldwide renown. Violet powder was long popular in the 19th century. It was made from starch, orris root, lemon, bergamot and oil of cloves (carmine or cochineal). Rose powder for the face consisted of rice starch, rouge, rose and sandalwood oil. As well as rice and wheat starch, nut starch (from almonds, pistachios and Brazil nuts) was also favoured on account of its fineness. A powder that was much prized was made with pistachio starch and fine chalk as the basis with rose and lavender oil to give scent. Finally there were countless powders with a talc basis. In the 18th century the scenting of powder was achieved through the "enfleurage des poudres" technique. Freshly gathered flower material was packed into air tight containers with one or two bases (starch, chalk, talc, finely ground orris root or ambergris, milled oak moss and tartar). After a certain time the wilted flowers were removed by sieving and replaced by fresh material until the powder had reached the desired strength of fragrance. Jasmine, jonquil, orange blossom, rose petals, lily of the valley and tuberose were used. The scentless components (e. g. ambergris or oakmoss) served as fixatives. The most unusual and one could say the most unhealthy use of perfumed powders occurred in France, where instead of being fumigated apartments were powdered by means of bellows. The ageing Richelieu is said have asked for it particularly.

PERFUMED GLOVES

Everyone who uses perfume knows that it should be applied to skin and not to clothes. It is, therefore, perhaps difficult to understand why perfumed gloves should have played such a disproportionately great role in the history of scent. The main reason must have been the aversion most people have for the smell of newly tanned leather but one cannot exclude the possibility that the impregnation of gloves with musk and other aromatic materials was of prophylactic intention.

The custom began at the Florentine court in the 16th century. Isabella d'Este is credited with the invention of glove perfumes. The fashion is said to have been imported to France by Catherine de Medici and her personal perfumer René.

In Florence perfumed gloves were highly prized gifts, and if they were not only treated with perfume but also with poison they were both pleasant and useful adjuncts to internecine strife. The fact that the unpleasant smell of leather should have led the art of perfumery to a highpoint of refinement in France is not without its irony. In fact it was the honourable company of glovers, established in the 12th century, which obtained letters patent from Louis XIV (in 1656) allowing them to be called "tant maîtres gantiers que parfumeurs". The guild was privileged to manufacture gloves and related

items in leather and, as perfumers, to treat them with aromatic substances, and had the right, indeed the monopoly, to deal in perfumes of all kinds.

These gloves cannot have been very appetising, the insides being smeared with a fatty substance containing musk, ambergris or civet, all of these ingredients having an unpleasant smell when concentrated. This application served a secondary purpose, that of keeping the leather soft.

As the fashion spread in 17th century England, they appeared to have devised better recipes. It would otherwise be difficult to explain why the Countess of Pembroke had the amazing quantity of 99 pairs of gloves delivered from Paris in 1622. It is reported that leather was improved in the 18th century, and indeed earlier, with the "enfleurage des poudres" method explained elsewhere. According to an English recipe, leather gloves were washed, dried and then immersed in rosewater. After being dried again, they were treated with a six day old mixture of oil of almonds, storax, pounded white lily root (probably orris) and then dried once more.

No other monarch dressed as splendidly as Elizabeth I of England, as many paintings of the queen demonstrate. It is no wonder that Edward de Vere, Earl of Oxford, stood high in her favour, for he had brought back from Italy for his sovereign, among a wealth of other presents, a scented leather garment and perfumed gloves. Her joy at this latter gift is said to be evident in a portrait in which she displays the gloves with arms outstretched. A pair of her gloves is still to be seen in the Bodleian Library in Oxford. At court they still spoke years afterwards of "the Earl of Oxford's perfume".

Perfumed gloves were not restricted to the Royal court. In the 17th century they were an intrinsic part of every perfumers's stock. They were sold under the name of "Roman gloves" and smelt of jasmine, neroli or the famous frangipani. According to Samuel Pepys some gloves were sold in walnut shells: they must have been made of very fine leather (goose skin?) indeed!

BERGAMOT BOXES AND PATCH BOXES

These charming boxes (Fig. 36) are among the rarer curiosities of perfume history and were, as far as we know, in the form described below, made exclusively in Grasse in the South of France. As holders for perfume bottles they could be seen as forerunners of today's packaging. It is, however, not clear whether they were sold containing bottles; they possibly also held perfumed soap.

The method of making them was as follows: the skin of the carefully peeled bergamot fruit was turned inside out and pressed over a prepared form, and left until it was completely dry and hard. It was then covered with a thin layer of paper the surface of which was subsequently treated with chalk and glue and then polished. The painted decoration was added and then slightly coloured varnish applied.

Similar in style to other forms of folk painting – peasant, religious art of the period, for example – the naive decoration on these boxes shows the symbols of love then popular, the flaming heart, Eros with bow and arrow, or putti in a primitively painted landscape.

There is great variety in the shape of the boxes; round, heart shaped, animal shaped as, for example, the cockerel in Fig. 35. A spherical box in the Musée de Grasse is particularly attractive. It shows a hunting scene and each of its "hemispheres" comes from the same fruit. It was no doubt intended as a soap holder. Some examples have a relief portrait on the lid and real beauties are in the form of figures or groups of figures, which in their execution recall Neapolitan crib figures. Well known people in public life are often represented, or everyday, often embarrassing, events. One might come across Lord Nelson, Napoleon in his typical pose, a drummer boy, a girl at the well (Fig. 37), or even an apothecary administering a purge – all expressions of a naive, quaint folk art which shines brightly in gay colours.

Fig. 35   Bergamot box in the form of a cock. France, early 19th Ct. Drawn after an original in the Musée de Grasse.

Among the many boxes and containers which have been used in connection with perfume and cosmetics one deserves our particular attention. Its contents, patches or "mouches" were one of the marks of female, but not always only female, vanity and served, along with perfume and cosmetics, the cause of sexual conquest and, if this indeed took place, the continuity of the resulting liaison.

Such patch boxes were not only found in the vicinity of the scent bottle but were often combined with it. This type of dual use container made it possible to have patches and perfume at hand when abroad, in addition to other beauty necessities. If not used for patches, the container might hold rouge or some other form of makeup. They were too small to serve as powder boxes. If the compartment attached to the scent bottle were not used for any of the aforementioned items, sweets or any kind of pill, especially breath sweetening cachous might be stored there. In the example in Illustration 282 an additional feature is built into the lid of the container: that supreme aid to vanity, the mirror.

Where and when the curious fashion of wearing patches was first adopted is unclear. The earliest patch box in England is dated 1669. It is supposed that possibly a decade earlier some court beauty had the idea of sticking a leather plaster over some facial flaw or other to hide it in the way her modern counterpart would use a cover fluid or stick. This evidently caused such a stir – for such a patch could by no means be overlooked – that she then made it part of her stock-in-trade. Only feminine guile could turn a defect into an attraction, or draw attention to a non existent one to the same effect. It was not long before the idea was copied. The wearing of patches made of pieces of

Fig. 36   Bergamot box in the form of a lidded basket. Ivory coloured and painted with flowers. France, early 19th Ct. Parfumerie Fragonard, Grasse

Fig. 37   Bergamot box in the form of a girl at a fountain. France, early 19th Ct. Drawn after an original in the Musée de Grasse.

thin leather or cloth spread like wildfire through the whole of Europe. That this is no exaggeration is proved by an entry in Pepys diary which speaks of the Duchess of Newcastle wearing many patches around her mouth on account of an outbreak of spots.

As is the case with every fashion, it was taken to extremes. Soon it was not only simple patches which were worn, but patches of every design: sun, moon and stars (the moon in all its phases) were displayed on many a visage. Eugene Rimmel depicts a young lady who even had the silhouette of a team of horses on her forehead; sailing ships and landscapes were not unknown. In France patches were known as "flies in the milk" (mouches). The language of patches was developed: according to the position of the patch of the face it could be read as "la passionnée" (at the corner of the eye), "la baiserie" (at the corner of the mouth), "la galante" (on the cheek); if in the décolleté of the chalk white bosom, it was referred to as "la révéleuse". Connoisseurs of amorous delights could discover patches on parts of the body not normally seen in public. The latter fact makes clear to us why German moralists thundered against this base custom and why the puritan fanatics introduced a bill in England in 1650 against "the vice of painting and wearing black patches and immodest dress in women". It did not make it to the statute book and the ladies of the land went from excess to excess; and later, in the 18th century, even politics entered the vanity game: ladies, perhaps gentlemen too, who supported the Conservatives wore their patches on the left cheek and those in favour of the Whigs on the right.

"Collecting has the value of sport" wrote the German poet Joachim Ringelnatz, and collecting is indeed not merely a pastime which is a source of pleasure to many people, but a passion pursued by some with the same amount of dedication that a sportsman will train for his sport. But is it merely a pastime, an escape from reality into a world that is past? Hardly, for if collecting were pointless, the many private collections and indeed the great public museums would have no raison d'etre.

Every object made by the hand of man, even the simplest everyday item, has artistic merit. In the case of perfume containers the practical is perfectly combined with the beautiful; many can rank as small works of art. They reflect the high value of their contents and are a witness to the ability of craftsmen down the centuries. In form and execution they reflect every period and are an insight into the historical, sociological and even religious background of the time in which they were made and used. It must be acknowledged, however, that in every era, including to a certain extent those of recent memory, and, indeed our own, luxury items were a testimony to the way of life of the higher échelons of society only.

The mere acquisition of countless objects results only in a pointless accumulation. In a true – and ideal – collection, on the other hand – perfume containers will, therefore, be shown in their natural habitat, that is, in the context of the style in dress and living of their period. Highly specialised collections of objects of any kind can easily become boring and uninformative. In the case of perfume, as the illustrations in this book show, there are containers in such a variety of form, the design sometimes effectively disguising the function, that any collection must be enhanced by their inclusion. Scent bottles alone could be used to demonstrate the history of metalwork, porcelain and glass. For this reason we find that the collections of the great museums are spread out in the various departments and not exhibited together. Collections of scent bottles alone are rare, usually private and not easily accessible to the general public. Two German cosmetic manufacturers have created museums open to the public showing scent containers in connection with hygiene and beauty care (the Schwarzkopf Collection in Steinhorst near Hamburg, and the Wella Collection in Darmstadt). In doing so they have shown an understanding of modern museum techniques in an exemplary fashion.

Collecting scent bottles

Fig. 38 Perfume spray ring. By pressing a rubber bulb beneath the finger a spray of perfume is released into the air. England, 2nd h. 19th Ct. From Piesse: The Art of Perfumery, 1879

Fig. 39 Commercial flacon in form of roller-skates. Colourless pressed glass with diamond mark "Deposé" and dated 11 February 1876. England. Collection Dr. Ian MacDougall

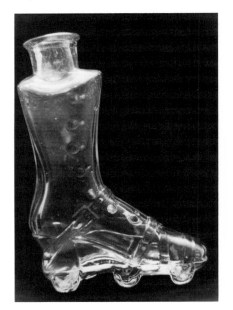

IN THE NAME OF BEAUTY: THE SCHWARZKOPF COLLECTION
by Maria Jedding-Gesterling

Fig. 40 "Habit de Parfumeur" Hand coloured copper engraving by Gerrit Valck, printed by N. de L'Armessin, Paris 1697. 370 × 243 mm. With a smoking brûle-parfum on his head, the perfumer offers on his tray all kinds of delights, for example essences of every type, pomades, scented water, perfumed powders and soaps, pastilles for sweetening the breath, pastilles for burning, rouge and perfumed (Spanish) leather. C. Schwarzkopf

There was always a close link between perfume and beauty care, thus a part of the Schwarzkopf Collection is dedicated to this theme: ancient balsam containers, scent bottles, smelling boxes, brûle-parfums and pot pourris are among the most imaginative and in craftsmanship the finest artefacts that our ancestors found essential in their attentions to personal hygiene and beauty.

Whereas these objects are associated with the sense of smell, many of the other utensils and tools in the Schwarzkopf Collection are rather connected with the beauty and grooming of the outward appearance. Hair and beard care, the fashion for the occasionally soft pink, at other times pale waxy complexion, the manicure, and body care in general were already drawing inventiveness from the Egyptians and Sumerians five thousand years ago. Cosmetic dishes, bronze razors, figures of gods and portraits tell us something about the body hygiene of that period and especially of the scented bath which was of prime importance in all beauty care. The word cosmetic comes from the Greek and many beauty recipes have their origin in the arts practised by the Arab, Egyptian and Greek ladies of their time. White foundation makeup, rouge for the cheeks, lip colour, the darkening of eyelashes and eyebrows are not inventions of recent times.

At all times man has been concerned with his personal appearance, it being a reflection of his approach to life, his social position, or his attempts to arrive at such a position. He could either go along with the current accepted fashion in his external appearance or adopt provocative nonconformist tendencies. Political upheaval and social change have always been mirrored in the fashions of the day, perhaps in that old styles of dress fell from grace, that extravagance ended up at the guillotine, or in that new rulers meant new styles to copy.

The Schwarzkopf Collection opens our eyes to the subtle changes in human appearance and lifestyle down the centuries. It presents an outline of history which is pleasing to look at, focussing on an intimate area of human activity, that which is concerned with man's need to show himself in the best light and his daily battle with nature's restrictions: the body he has received and the ageing process.

Why should a cosmetic firm such as Hans Schwarzkopf Ltd. establish a museum for the social and cultural history of hair and beauty care? When the foundations for this undertaking were laid in the 1930s the intention was to show the firm's connection with the hairdressing trade. The tools and preparations of the wigmakers and barbers gave, and still give aspiring hairdressers, whose training is of great concern to the firm, an insight into the history of their trade. Only in our century has beauty care become less of a privilege, but more the normal practice for the average person. Through innovative developments such as the alkali-free shampoo and the cold permanent wave, the firm of Schwarzkopf contributed towards making modern hair care less time consuming, less expensive and more beneficial to

87

the hair itself. It is the intention of the firm to illustrate such developments by means of its exhibits in the museum, and draw our attention to times in history when beauty products and accessories were beyond the means of the less well-off.

The manor house of Steinhorst in the "Duchy of Lauerburg (Schleswig Holstein) Collection" has shown a similar history of initial exclusiveness to aristocratic circles then later accessibility to the public. It was built in 1721 at the behest of the Gottfried von Wedderkop, Lord of the Manor and ambassador and was the nerve centre of a noble estate. It was purchased and restored in 1976 by Schwarzkopf and opened as a training centre for hairdressers, employees of the firm, and other interested firms and associations. As the headquarters of the "Duchy of Lauenburg Foundation" it is also the office for the protection of the cultural heritage of the area. The Schwarzkopf Collection is given an ideal setting in eight rooms decorated in 18th century style. The manor house, built at a time when perfume, powder and cosmetics were of prime importance, is a particularly suitable home for the perfume container collection, and also allows us to scent the spirit of the late Baroque in the countless beauty accessories of that period exhibited here.

Professionally supervised, the collection is not only available to the general public at Steinhorst, but often goes on its travels to special exhibitions in other parts of Germany and neighbouring countries.

List of Abbreviations

c.	*circa*
Ct.	*Century*
D.	*Diameter*
f. l. to r.	*From left to right*
h.	*Half*
H.	*Height*
L	*Length*
qu.	*Quarter*
W.	*Width*
BM	*British Museum, London*
BNM	*Bayerisches Nationalmuseum, Munich*
CG	*Collection Godfrey, Leeds*
C. Schwarz-kopf	*Collection Schwarzkopf, Steinhorst*
KGMB	*Kunstgewerbemuseum, Berlin (West)*
KGMK	*Kunstgewerbemuseum, Köln (Cologne)*
KHMW	*Kunsthistorisches Museum, Wien (Vienna)*
LM	*London Museum*
MAKW	*Museum für Angewandte Kunst, Wien (Vienna)*
MKG	*Museum für Kunst und Gewerbe, Hamburg*
MKG/CB	*Museum für Kunst und Gewerbe, Hamburg (Collection Blohm)*
P	*Private Collection (Hastings, London, Munich etc)*
PG	*Private Collection G, Amsterdam*
PR	*Private Collection R*
R	*Rosenborg, Copenhagen*
RA	*Rijksmuseum, Amsterdam*
RGM	*Römisch-Germanisches Museum, Köln (Cologne)*
V. & A.	*Victoria & Albert Museum, London*

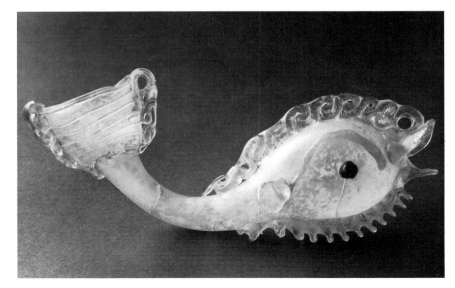

◁ *Fig. 41 Scent container in the form of a dolphin. Colourless glass with blue and black details. Edges with pincered decoration. Dorsal fin with glass threads. Roman, 2–3rd Ct. AD. RGM*

1 Small amphora, alabastron and oenochoe. Vessels for balm. Sand-core glass. Eastern Mediterranean, 3–2nd Ct. B. C. H. (l. to r.) 88, 100, 90 mm. C. Schwarzkopf.

2 Head-shaped vessel. Bronze. Etruria. End of 3rd Ct. B. C. H. 100 mm. Balsamarium for aromatic oils, burial object for females. Goddess of beauty with "melon hairstyle", wearing diadem, earrings and neck ornament. Side rings for chain; stopper extant. C. Schwarzkopf.

To page 91:
3 Bottle in fish-shape. Bronze. Persia. 9th Ct. B. C. H. 99 mm. C. Schwarzkopf.

4 Bottle in female form wearing wig-like headdress. Bronze. Greek, c. 800 B.C. H. 98 mm. C. Schwarzkopf.

5 Alabastron for unguent or balm. Alabaster. Egypt. 2nd Ct. B. C. H. 85 mm. C. Schwarzkopf.

3 △

4 ▽

6 △   7 ▽

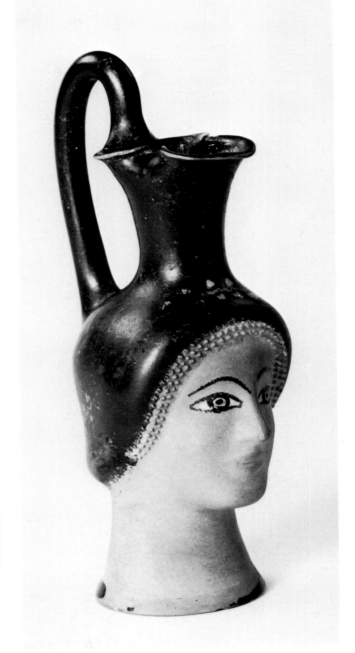

To page 92:

6 Balsamarium in form of an astragal (ankle joint) with knot handle. Terracotta with black glaze. Southern Italy 4th Ct. B.C. H. 65 mm. C. Schwarzkopf.

7 Askos. Terracotta, red ground with black glaze. Decorated with two goat motifs. Greece 5–4th Ct. B.C. H. 56 mm. C. Schwarzkopf.

8 Clover-leaf jug in form of woman's head. Light brown terracotta with black glaze. Attic. 1st qu. 5th Ct. B.C. H. 170 mm. C. Schwarzkopf.

9 Ram balsamarium. Light brown terracotta with matt black and dark purple painting. Etrusco-Corinthian, 6th Ct. B.C. H. 50 mm. The left ear is the vessel's opening. C. Schwarzkopf. ▷

10 Three scent bottles: a helmeted head, a female bust and a horse's head. All terracotta with partial blue glazing. Rhodes, c. 580 B.C. H. (l. to r.) 65, 120, 75 mm. BM ▽

11 △   14 ▽   12 △   15 ▽   13 △   16 ▽

94

To page 94:

11 Relief-lekythos with scene from the nuptial chamber. Light brown terracotta with black glaze. Attic. 4th Ct. B. C. H. 127 mm. C. Schwarzkopf.

12 Small Lekythos. Ochre-coloured terracotta with black painting on a white ground. Attic, c. 450 B. C. H. 84 mm. The painting shows a mounted warrior attacked by two foot soldiers armed with shields and lances. C. Schwarzkopf.

13 Round-shouldered lekythos. Ochre-coloured terracotta with black varnish. Apulia, 370–350 B. C. H. 185 mm. Lady in long gown at her toilette, holding a mirror in her right hand. Protected by a female slave. She faces a naked youth bearing a staff, wreath and cloak. C. Schwarzkopf.

14 Alabastron with narrow neck. Rosette decoration and lion motif in black and purple paint on light brown terracotta. Early Corinthian, c. 600 B. C. H. 150 mm. C. Schwarzkopf.

15 Lekythos. Terracotta, red ground with black glaze. Attic, c. 450 B. C. H. 330 mm. Decoration: female slave with toilet box and balsamarium. C. Schwarzkopf.

16 Lekythos with scene of lady at her toilette. Terracotta, red ground with black glaze, c. 450 B. C. H. 330 mm. The lady holds her mirror with both hands, the servant passes the cosmetic holder. C. Schwarzkopf.

17 Alabastron with toilette scene and geometric friezes below the flared opening and at base. Terracotta, white ground. Attic, made and signed by Passiades, 510–500 B. C. H. 144 mm. The loosely clad woman holds an unguent dish in her outstretched hand. BM ▷

19 △   20 ▽

Incense containers

21 Incense burner with foot and suspension ring for chain. Upper part architectural in structure resembling a chapel, pierced. Bronze, partially gilded. Western Germany. 12th Ct. H. 210 mm. MKG ▷

To page 96:
18 Glass bottle, mould blown bottle in the shape of a head, flat base, long neck, and Greek inscription. Iridiscent through burial. Cyprus from a grave near Idalion; probably made in Syria 1st Ct. B.C. H. 198 mm. BM

19 Bottle with two handles on shoulder and relief of a helmeted head. Lead. Roman Empire. H. 90 mm. C. Schwarzkopf.

20 Balsamarium with two handles connecting rim and shoulder. Blown glass with weathering crust, the chips revealing iridiscent surfaces. Roman Empire. H. 122 mm. C. Schwarzkopf.

22 △

23 △

24 ▽

To page 98:

22 Romanesque incense burner without foot. Upper part has pierced decoration in four segments, symmetrical stylised leaf motifs. Bronze. Germany, early 12th Ct. H. 125 mm. V. & A.

23 Incense burner with dish-like lower part on a wide foot and attached chains. Pierced upper part of architectural construction after a design for a cathedral chapel. Gilded silver, silver chains with terminal plate and suspension ring. English 2nd qu. 14th Ct. H. 275 mm. V. & A.

24 Navicula, boat-shaped incense holder on a hexagonal foot, hinged lid with knob. Upper edges crenellated and terminating at each end in rams' heads. Gilded silver. England, early 14th Ct. H. 125 mm. V. & A. The objects in Ill. 23 and 24 formed part of the Ramsey Abbey (Huntingdonshire) treasure. Probably lost at the time of the Reformation they were recovered from Whittlesea Mere in 1850, along with pewter plates bearing the ram's head motif – the Abbey's rebus – when the Mere was drained.

25 △

26 ▽

25 Fume pot. Stoneware with brown-green glazing. England. Excavated in Southampton, 17th Ct. H. 120 mm. Southampton Museum.

26 Fume pot. Stoneware with light green glazing. England. Excavated at Southampton. Late 16th Ct. H. 220 mm. Southampton Museum.

Brûle-parfums

◁ 27 Brûle-parfum with heavy bowl-like lower part on claw feet with rich decoration in the mannerist style. The partially pierced upper part with elaborate figure and foliage ornament and furnished with a balustrade where it meets the lower is crowned with a martial figure. Silver. Spain, c. 1630. H. 230 mm. V. & A.

28 Brûle-parfum with removable burner on a tripod base. Silver. Lithuania, Reval, c. 1750. H. 165 mm. C. Schwarzkopf. ▽

29 Brûle-parfum. Bronze, gilt. France, end of 18th century. H. 240 mm. Three curved legs bear the cauldron-like vessel which contains a small compartment for aromatic substances which when heated in it give off their scent through the pierced lid. C. Schwarzkopf.

30 Brûle-parfum. Brass, fire-gilded. Origin uncertain, c. 1800. The egg-shaped container has a turned wooden stopper in the opening. Three curved pipes screwed into the top distribute the scent. It is supported by four pierced metal strips, one of which is hinged to allow for fuelling the burner. Chained tweezers facilitate the introduction of flowers and herbs. C. Schwarzkopf.

31 Brûle-parfum in black hyalith glass with gilt decoration. Chinaman in bronze with enamel colours. Gold mount. Wooden box with drawer for perfume burning tools forms the base. Inside a platinum catalyser. The scent emerges from the Chinaman's mouth. Southern Bohemia, c. 1830. H. 185 mm. P. Frankfurt.

32 Brûle-parfum. Column-like design, the lower half with vertical ridges contrasting with the flower decoration of the upper. Pressed glass stopper in the form of a girl. Colourless glass with matt surface. France, René Lalique, early 20th Ct. H. 210 mm. P. Frankfurt.

 29 △   30 ▽   31   32

34 Brûle-parfum. The Sitting Buddha figure, also referred to as a "pagoda". The lower part of the back open for the insertion of perfumed candles, the smoke emerging from the open mouth. Porcelain. Germany, Meissen, before 1720. BM

◁ 33 Brûle-parfum. Porcelain. Germany, Meissen, c. 1750. H. 245 mm. Three putti standing on a rocaille structure hold a circular base into which an urn-shaped perfume container is inserted. Two helmeted heads on the shoulder of the urn act as handles; the front and rear show classical relief heads wearing laurel wreaths. The scent intensified through the heat from the burning of the spirit emanates from the pierced lid. C. Schwarzkopf.

35 Pot-pourri vase with three putti. Painted
porcelain. Germany, Meissen, 1760–1774.
H. 164 mm. Coloured painted garlands and
gold highlighting. In relief: four dancing
nymphs and two putti with goat in front of a
statue. C. Schwarzkopf.

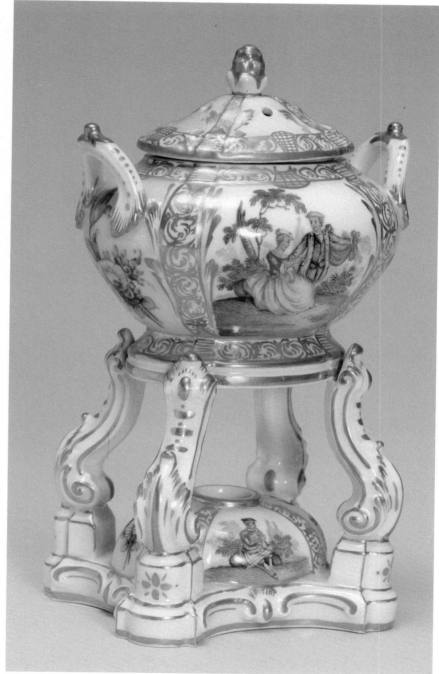

36 Brûle-parfum. Porcelain with genre
scenes, flower painting and gold decoration.
Germany, Königliche Porzellanmanufak-
tur Berlin; painted by Helena Wolfsohn,
Dresden, late 19th century. H. 165 mm.
C. Schwarzkopf.   ▷

38 △   39 ▽

Pot-pourris

40 Pot-pourri with three putti between roses. Rich flower painting, lavish rocaille decor in red and gold. Porcelain. Germany, Höchst, c. 1770. H. 385 mm. MKG

41 Pot-pourri with pierced rocaille ornament. Landscape painting with lady and two gentlemen. Porcelain. Germany, Fürstenberg, c. 1765. H. 280 mm. MKG

42 Pot-pourri with two handles and pierced below the rim. Flower arrangements in red, yellow, violet and blue surrounded by a wine-red leaf pattern; rosebud finial. Faience. France, Strasburg, Joseph Hannong, c. 1765. H. 235 mm. MKG

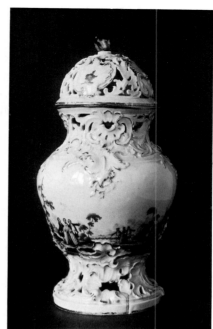

40 △   41 △   42 ▽

To page 104:

37 Pot-pourri on three feet with relief heads, flower painting and garlands. Lid with circular opening. Porcelain. Germany, Ludwigsburg, c. 1760. H. 230 mm. C. Schwarzkopf.

38 Pot-pourri. Gilt bronze and green cut glass. Paris c. 1850. H. 365 mm. The two halves of the pineapple-like fruit open when the ape finial is pressed revealing an apple-shaped pierced perfume container. C. Schwarzkopf.

39 Pot-pourri with pierced body and lid. Porcelain. France, Mennecy, 18th Ct. H. 205 mm. C. Schwarzkopf.

Pomanders

43 Pendant pomander in gilded silver; probably part of a rosary. Spherical body with two-layered tracery work. Flower rosettes and suspensory rings at top and bottom. Germany. 2nd half 15th Ct. H. 27 mm. V. & A.

44 Pendant pomander in gilded silver. Body separating into six segments. Segment lids and central column surfaces numbered in Roman figures. Screw lid with flat pierced eyelet and ring. Outer walls decorated with flower and fruit motifs and trailing ribbons. England, late 17th Ct. H. 48 mm. V. & A.

45 Pomander in silver with black enamelling, on a slightly domed foot. Separating into six segments. Outer wall with stylised plant motifs; leaf frieze around the foot. Ornamental eyelet and ring. Screw cap with rosette pattern and pearl edge. England. 1st h. 17th Ct. H. 49 mm. V. & A.

46 Pendant pomander in gilded silver. Compressed spherical shape. The two halves, separated by a twisted wire, pierced and decorated with filigree work. Top and bottom with rosettes and knob-like finials. Probably a rosary attachment. Spain, 17th Ct. H. 15 mm. V. & A.

43 △   45 ▽   44 △   46 ▽

To page 107:
49 Pomander in gilded silver with enamel decoration. Dividing into four segments. Figure of Madonna and Child in the central column. Sliding lids on the segments and the sides with figures of saints (Dorothy, John, Barbara, Andrew, Mary Magdalene, Paul, Catherine and Peter) in low relief, and with motto bands. Outer wall with curling motto bands and pierced decoration below the sky with sun and cloud. Has the appearance of a "Betnuss" when closed. Germany (Rhenish master?), c. 1500. H. 50 mm. BNM

47 Pomander on a flat foot. Silver with niello decoration. Body in six segments. Outer wall decorated in the style of the Netherlands artist Michel le Blon (1587–1660). Central six-sided column forming another compartment, which is open below and standing on the circular pierced foot. Holland, early 17th Ct. H. 34 mm. V. & A.

48 Pomander in gilded silver similar in shape to a smelling box. Rhombic in outline with the centre forming a hollow tetrahedron (this pierced and with formal leaf decoration). Edges with a wide band of decoration of chiselled foliage work. Hinged lid closed with a hook below. Ball finial with suspensory ring. Germany, late 16th Ct. H. 50 mm. V. & A.

47 △   48 △   49 ▽

50, 51 Pomander. Silver, inside gilded. Germany, 16th Ct. H. 50 mm. When unscrewed the pomander collapses into eight segments, the sliding lids of which bear the names of the contents: 1. "KANEL", 2. "SCHLAG", 3. "ROSMARIN", 4. "MUSCAT", 5. "NEGELKEN", 6. "ROSEN", 7. "CITRON", 8. "LAVENDEL" (resp. cinnamon, musk, rosemary, nutmeg, cloves, rose, lemon peel, lavender). A small spoon is attached to the foot which screws off. The closed pomander is decorated with four medallion-shaped panels each enclosing a bird motif. C. Schwarzkopf.

52, 53 Pomander on a disc-like foot. Silver. Body divided into six segments. Outer decoration in pierced foliage work. On a similar but smaller sphere cupid with arrow. Sides of the segments with foliage work. Germany, 2nd h. 17th Ct. H. 74 mm. V. & A.

50 △   52 ▽   51 △   53 ▽

54, 55 Pomander combined with watch dial. Silver and bronze with watch glass. Ill. 54: the dial with fixed hand and encircling pierced foliage work; hinge visible above. Ill. 55: opened to reveal four compartments for aromatic material. England, 17th Ct. D. 28 mm. W. 17 mm. LM

56 Cross – shaped combined perfume pendant in silver. Cylindrical body below the loop with four chambers and screw closures; below unscrewable spray attachment for liquid perfume (perfumed vinegar). Loop and suspensory ring. England, 17th Ct. H. 70 mm. V. & A.

57, 58 Scent container pendant in the form of toad on a leaf. Silver gilt, the hollow body divided horizontally into three compartments; on the lid the inscriptions "Schlag B", "Cannel B", "Citron B" (see Ill. 50/51). Ill. 57: under side of the leaf with pierced decorated lid. Germany, 17th Ct., L. (Leaf) 32 mm. V. & A.

54 △

56 ▽

55 △

57 ▽

58 ▽

59 Rosary-like ornament with pomanders in the form of a queen's head and skulls. Coral, gold enamelled and set with rubies and table-cut gems. Germany(?), 17th Ct. L. 250 mm. CR

60, 61, 62 Double-faced pendant pomander. Front side: Face of young woman with inscription "SUM" (I am) around throat. Rear: a death's head with inscription "FUI" (I was i.e. I am no more). Eye sockets open to the inside. Hinge underneath; screw fastener on top. Four open compartments inside. Silver gilt. Germany, 16th Ct. H. 30 mm. P. Munich.

60 △

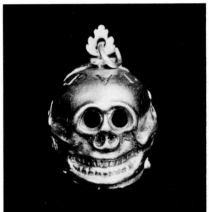

61 △

62 ▽

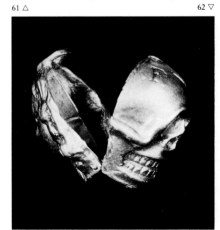

◁ 63 Carved meditational nut. Boxwood with hollow silver sphere containing relief carvings of Mary and Child and John the Evangelist. Northwest Germany, c. 1500. D. 57 mm. MKG

64 Carved meditational nut with chain. Walnut, silver gilt mount. Sweden, c. 1660. D. 37 mm. Relief bust of Carolus Gustavus Rex (Sweden 1654–1660) above the coat of arms of Sweden and Norway, also David's triumph over Goliath. The inscription "Si Deus pro nobis quis contra nos" on a lid of the metal inset. MKG

65 Meditational nut. Boxwood with copper gilt capsule. Flanders, Adam Dirksz, c. 1500. D. 41 mm. Pyramus and Thisbe and Abraham's Sacrifice carved in the wood. Interior metal capsule with crucifixion. Mass of St. Gregory and around the rim the Lamentations of Jeremiah. MKG

64 △

65 ▽

◁ ◁ 66 Snailshell pomander. Silver. Germany, c. 1700. D. 23 mm. The container has both a pierced and a closed side which open clam-like. C. Schwarzkopf.

◁ 67 Bell-shaped pomander, two-layered with suspensory ring. Gold with coloured enamel decoration and set with pearls. Inner and outer walls filigree-like and with flower and foliage motifs; upper and lower parts separated by a concave decorative band also set with pearls. Pearl hanging from the bottom. South Germany, late 16th Ct. H. 70 mm. V. & A. This pomander was probably part of a rosary.

◁ 68 Perfumed cushion. Cushion covered with rough cloth, set on a dish and surmounted by the half-figure of a worthy matron. Silver gilt. Germany, Munich, Caspar Wendl, c. 1620. H. 60 mm. P. Munich.

69 △

70

71 △

72 △

73 ▽

74 ▽

69–74 Smelling box as puzzle egg. The ivory egg conceals a golden egg (Ill. 69, 70) and from this hatches a golden hen set with diamonds (Ill. 71, 72) which in turn contains a golden crown (Ill. 73). This conceals a diamond ring with monogram (Ill. 74). Gift from Christian VII (1749–1808) of Denmark to his Queen Caroline Mathilde (of England). CR

75 △

76 △

77 △

78 ▽

79 ▽

To page 114:

75 Barrel-shaped smelling box. Porcelain, hinged lid and mount in gilt brass. Germany, Meissen, c. 1730/40. H. 29 mm. Battle scenes with mounted soldiers surrounded by vermilion medallions. Flower painting on the base. Lid with bunch of flowers in relief. MKG/CB

76 Smelling box in the shape of an egg, with relief rocailles and coloured scattered flowers. Porcelain, copper mount. Germany, Meissen, c. 1760. H. 31 mm. MKG

77 Smelling box in the shape of an egg, with rustic roses, forget-me-nots and asters. Enamel, engraved copper mount with pierced inner lid. Germany, mid 18th Ct. H. 37 mm. MGK/CB

78 Smelling box combined with a seal. Silver. Holland, early 18th Ct. H. 28 mm. V. & A.

79 Smelling box in the shape of an egg, unscrews into two parts. Brass. Germany, beginning 18th Ct. H. 30 mm. C. Schwarzkopf.

80 △   81 ▽   82 ▽

80 Double gourd-shaped smelling box with curving silver stopper and suspensory ring. The hinge for the lid just visible. Copper or silver, pale blue enamelled with applied flower decoration in silver. Germany, Berlin or Augsburg, early 18th Ct. H. 45 mm. Städtische Kunstsammlungen Augsburg.

81 Smelling box in twig-with-pear design. Three detachable scent containers. Silver, gilt inside. Germany, Augsburg, beginning of 18th Ct. H. 75 mm. A domed pierced holder is concealed in the large fruit. C. Schwarzkopf.

82 Pear-shaped smelling box, covered with a mass of filigree flowers. Silver, partly gilt. South Germany, c. 1700. H. 90 mm. Flips open in the middle. Twig with leaves unscrews. C. Schwarzkopf.

83 Smelling box in the shape of a pilgrim's bottle on a conical ring-foot. Silver gilt. The concave front is removable to facilitate the insertion of a sponge soaked in aromatic substances. When closed it is held in place by a push-on cap which is attached to a chain. Whereas the pierced front of the container displays a stylised flower motif the cap is engraved with a herringbone pattern. Holland, around 1680. H. 40 mm. V. & A.

84 Smelling box in the shape of a wickerwork flask. Silver, gilt inside. German, 1st h. 18th Ct. H. 73 mm. The box can be unscrewed at the top as well as near the bottom.

85 Smelling box in the shape of a pocket watch, with flower-like openwork internal lid. Silver, garnet in the centre. Owner's monogram "BM J. P. D." and maker's mark "WS". South German, 18/19th Ct. D. 28 mm. C. Schwarzkopf.

83 △   84 △   85 ▽

Facing page:
86 Egg-shaped smelling box, jasper in golden cagework; gilded inscription on white enamel rim, PAR FAVEUR CROIT L'AMOUR; release button set with diamond. French(?), 2nd h. 18th Ct. H. 48 mm. MKG/CB

87 Gold vase-shaped flacon enriched with repoussé scrollwork and a mythological motif; Venus, with one bare breast is awaiting Adonis, beside her rests a greyhound. On the reverse a monkey is seen peeping through a scrollwork jungle. French, 1750/60. H. 83 mm. C. Schwarzkopf.

88 Pendant flacon, the cast and chased oval body takes the shape of a flattened urn on a small square foot and with a slender quadrangular neck, screw-top with loop; champlevé enamelled bosses on both sides. This flacon was most probably worn on a chain suspended from a belt. Spanish, around 1620. H. 83 mm. V. & A.

86 △

87 ▽

89 △

90 ▽

92 △

93 △

95 ▽

94 △

96 ▽

89 Scent bottle, cobalt-blue glass in cloisonné gilt cage. English(?), 1780–1800. H. 85 mm. P. London

90 Scent bottle, cobalt-blue glass encaged by golden scrollwork. English, 1780. H. 77 mm. P: London

91 Scent bottle, agate with chased gold mount. English, 1775–1785. H. 44 mm. MKG/CB

92, 93 Smelling boxes, silver. Ill. 92 with owner's monogram "MR". Frisian, 1772. H. 72 mm. C. Schwarzkopf. Ill. 93 with inset red glass stone. German, Flensburg, 1820. H. 70 mm. MKG

94, 95, 96 Smelling boxes with compartments for holding scented cushions. Silver, interior gilded. – Ill. 94: Danish, Copenhagen, Jens Sveistrup (around 1744–1826), dated 1767. H. 82 mm. C. Schwarzkopf. – Ill. 95: Owner's monogram "PM 1770", maker's mark "CFR", Danish, 1770. H. 75 mm. C. Schwarzkopf. – Ill. 96: Owner's monogram "M. L. B. B. S. L. D. 1784". Maker's mark "I S 82". German, Schleswig, 1782. H. 92 mm. MKG

97 Smelling box in the shape of a land snail. Shell surface with chiselled foliage work. Silver gilt. German, 18th Ct. V. & A.

98 Three smelling boxes in fish-shape. Silver, interior gilt (the carp also on the gills and fins), red glass eyes. North Germany, 2nd h. 18th Ct. The wide-mouthed fish with maker's mark "s" (L. 94 mm) and the carp (L. 83 mm) contain two scent containers, one in the head and the other within the body. The pike (L. 99 mm), made of thin silver has its mouth closed by later soldering. MKG

◁ 99

100 △

101 △

102 ▽

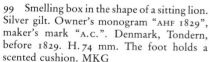

99 Smelling box in the shape of a sitting lion. Silver gilt. Owner's monogram "AHF 1829", maker's mark "A.C.". Denmark, Tondern, before 1829. H. 74 mm. The foot holds a scented cushion. MKG

100 Smelling box in the shape of an articulated fish, with painted papier mâché etui. Silver, fins and interior gilt, glass eyes. Denmark, Apenrade, end 18th Ct. L. 73 mm (fish), L. 82 mm (etui). MKG

101 As above. Silver, red glass eyes. Germany, Schwäbisch Gmünd, 2nd h. 18th Ct. L. 78 mm. C. Schwarzkopf.

102 As 100. Silver, red glass eyes. Maker's mark "HA". Germany, Schleswig, 18th Ct. L. 110 mm. C. Schwarzkopf.

⊲⊲ 103 Smelling box in the shape of a handled urn. Silver, interiors gilded, with three blue glass "gems". Owner's monogram "JJS 1836". Maker's mark "S". Denmark, before 1836. H. 90 mm. –The hollow foot opens with a hinged lid and holds a scented cushion.

⊲ 104 As above, with six large glass "gems" around the middle. The crown on the domed lid furnished with five small red glass "gems". Silver, interiors. Foot gilded within with owner's monogram "MPN GKS 1807" and maker's mark "SHG", holding scented cushion. Denmark, Apenrade, before 1807, H. 95 mm. C. Schwarzkopf.

⊲⊲ 105 Smelling box in the shape of a handled urn, decorated with flower garlands and with a seated cherub crowning the domed lid. Silver, interior gilded. Owner's monogram "F. E. H. 1820", maker's mark "HW". North Germany, before 1820 H. 92 mm. – The foot contains a compartment for a scented cushion. MKG

⊲ 106 Smelling box in form of a wardrobe. On the laterally hinged lid a cartouche showing a mother with two children, on the reverse a vase with flower garlands. Owner's monogram "GM" on underside, maker's mark "M. L. R." Germany, Emden, end 18th Ct. H. 43 mm. MKG

107 Smelling box. Red cut glass, copper mount with a pivoting disc beneath pierced lid. Bohemia, c. 1830/40. H. 29 mm. C. Schwarzkopf.

108 Smelling box resting on four ball feet. Lid and walls with openwork floral motifs. Silver. Europe, late 18th Ct. L. 102 mm. C. Schwarzkopf.

107 △

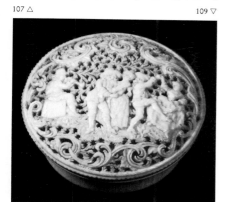

109 ▽

108 △

110 ▽

109 Smelling box. Lid in openwork depicting a dancing scene in the manner of Teniers. Ivory/France, Dieppe, middle 18th Ct. H. 27 mm, D. 60 mm. C. Schwarzkopf.

110 Vinaigrette with openwork grille. Silver, interior gilded. England, Birmingham 1830. L. 40 and 60 mm. C. Schwarzkopf.

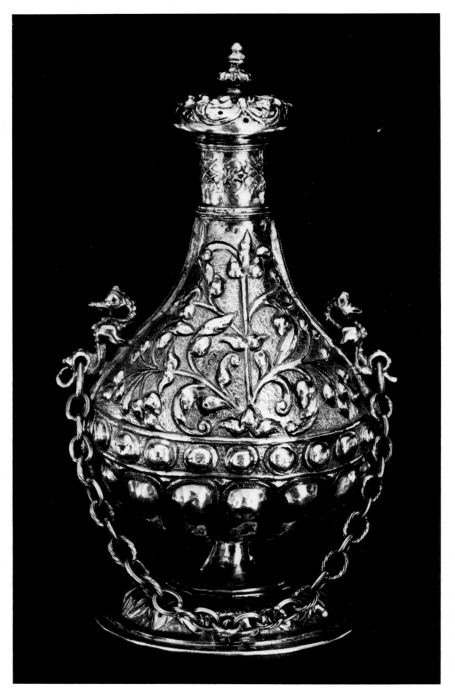

111 Repoussé casting bottle. Silver gilt. The pear-shaped body is decorated in the Mannerist style and rests on a wide-rimmed circular foot. Like similar pieces of this period this flacon has a pierced screw top. Although furnished with a chain attached to the shoulders of the vessel it was hardly carried around but had its place on the dinner, or perhaps more frequently, the toilet table. The decoration of stylised foliage work can be traced back to a sample book of Francesco Pellegrino which also served Hans Holbein when designing silver ware for Henry VIII. England 1553 H. 125 mm. Sotheby & Co. – A fine but later piece came recently to light together with other "objects of virtu", amongst them a gold-mounted glass scent bottle, from an orange box filled with wood shavings in an attic room of Burghley House (Stamford).

112 Flacon of compressed oval shape standing on a flat base; plain screw top; body delicately engraved with Cherubin, Lucretia and luxurious foliage work. Silver. England, late 17th Ct. V. & A.   ▷

113 Repoussé gold scent bottle with formal floral motifs, resting on a shallow foot. A lion's head on the right hand shoulder holds a chain which connects it with the screw top. England, late 17th Ct. H. 70 mm. P. London. A scent bottle similar in shape but with engraved decoration can be seen in B. Matthew's book (1973, fig. 43)   ▷ ▷

114 Extraordinarily richly embellished flacon with a suspensory chain, set with gems. Body and cap with decoration in enamel colours against a white background. Furnished with diamonds, rubies, topaz and small tablets of chalcedony engraved with a herringbone pattern, flat base, gold. England (most probably London), 16th or early 17th Ct. LM   ▷

115 Silver-gilt repoussé flacon on a wide-rimmed circular foot. The reliefs are based on themes by the painters Bartholomäus Sprengel and Hans von Aachen. Prague Court Workshop, 1580–1600. H. 130 mm. P. Munich.   ▷ ▷

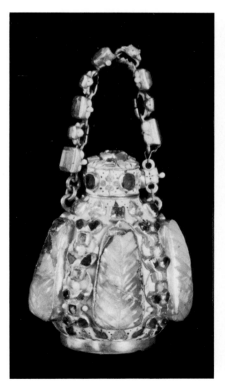 

◁◁ 116 Enamel flacon in the shape of a pilgrim's bottle, standing on a short flaring circular gilt foot, with suspensory rings on the shoulders and screw top. The front with a hinged lid opens to reveal a watch case the interior of which is painted with ruins in a landscape. The lid displays scenes in the manner of Teniers. France, 2nd h. 17th Ct. H. 56 mm. Sotheby & Co.

◁ 117 Flacon in the form of a pilgrim's flask. Gold with coloured enamel decoration and set with diamonds. Germany, Dresden, Johann Melchior Dinglinger. Early 18th Ct. H. 66 mm. CR

◁◁ 118 Flacon, standing on a circular seal-base. Silver. Decorated in enamel in front and on the reverse (half portrait of a stout lady wearing a red cloak). The rest of the flacon engraved with half moons and houses. Monogram of seal "LZ" France, 1st h. 18th Ct. H. 89 mm. C. Schwarzkopf.

◁ 119 Rock crystal flacon taking the form of a monstrance in elaborate silver gilt mounts. The richly decorated conical foot connected by a short column of rock crystal with the main body which is crowned on the lid by a figure fighting a lion. South German (Bavarian?) early 18th Ct. H. 120 mm. P. Munich.

120 Two-handled flacon standing on a flat circular foot. Silver gilt overlaid with open-work silver. Push-on stopper with globular amethyst finial. Germany, Magdeburg, 1st h. 18th Ct. H. 140 mm. P. Munich.

121 Scent bottle in the shape of a musical instrument. Silver gilt inlaid with mother-of-pearl. Engraved with figures of birds and rather coarse foliage motifs. The square foot functioned most probably as a seal. Lid with drop-shaped engraved finial. France or Netherlands. 2nd. h. 19th Ct. H. 87 mm – This scent bottle represents a typical example of the imitation of an older style (17th Ct.) in the period of Historism. ▷

122 △

123 △

124 △

122 Rock crystal scent bottle with a bust of Landgrave Carl of Hesse-Cassel forming the stopper and with a fine profile carving of his wife Marie-Amalie on the main body of the flacon. Germany, Cassel, C. Labhart, late 17th Ct. H. 157 mm. CR

123 Flacon of clear rock crystal with richly ornate silver-gilt mount, hinged lid with pearl finial. The stopper represents a bust of Bacchus. France. Late 17th or early 18th Ct. H. 110 mm. P. Munich.

124 Heart-shaped scent bottle suspended from a silver chatelain. Rock crystal, silver mount with castwork figures. Germany. 18th Ct. H. 150 mm (inl. chain). P. Munich.

◁ 125 Pendant flacon in the shape of an urn, with its original shagreen-covered etui. Carnelian, cut with star and diamonds. Gold mount with hinged lid above stopper. England(?) c. 1765. H. 43 mm. PG

126 Scent bottle with silver gilt mounts, standing on a flat base, cut and richly engraved with flower and foliage motifs, on one side a monogram beneath a crown. On underside of foot a seal with unidentified arms. Germany c. 1750. H. 79 mm. PG

127 Scent bottle of compressed oval shape. Rock crystal with richly decorated gold mounts. Stopper embellished with a Tudor rose. England, 18th Ct. H. 62 mm. PG ▷

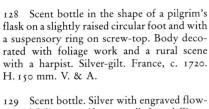

128 Scent bottle in the shape of a pilgrim's flask on a slightly raised circular foot and with a suspensory ring on screw-top. Body decorated with foliage work and a rural scene with a harpist. Silver-gilt. France, c. 1720. H. 150 mm. V. & A.

129 Scent bottle. Silver with engraved flower and foliage motifs; enamelled medallions. Stopper missing. Germany 2nd h. 17th Ct. H. 53 mm. – The medallion on the reverse depicts a striding angel with an hour glass on her head. Inscription reads "Hin Geht die Zeit" (tempus fugit) and "O Mensch Ihr Recht" (O Man your right). MKG

130 Pendant scent bottle. Gold, deep blue enamel and turmalin suspended on gold chains. France, 18th Ct. H. 65 mm. P. Munich.

131 Pendant scent bottle. Silver-gilt with cloisonné enamel decoration, set with garnets. Hungary (?) early 18th Ct. H. 70 mm. V. & A.

128 △   130 ▽   129 △   131 ▽

Facing page:

132 Flacon cum powder box. Brass-gilt. Maker's mark "LP". England, mid 19th Ct. H. 62 mm. Enamel medallion with portrait of a lady wearing a hat with three pearls. Powder puff with feathers and mounted on ivory. Flacon with brass-mounted cork stopper. C. Schwarzkopf.

133 Cone-shaped scent bottle. Silver set with agate of various colours. England, Birmingham, 2nd h. 19th Ct. L. 126 mm. PG

134 Flask-shaped scent bottle, lapis lazuli with richly decorated gold mount and a cameo on either side. Base of foot a lapis lazuli seal with forget-me-nots and the inscription "Ne m'oublie pas". France, 1760. H. 52 mm. PG

132 △

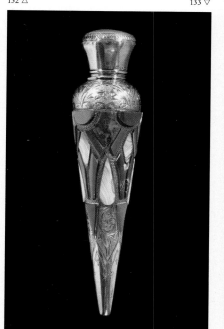

133 ▽

136 △   137 ▽

Facing page:

135 Scent bottle. Gold, enamelled, on both sides medallions "en camaieu" on a chocolate brown background. Gold screw top with vertical coloured broad enamel stripes. England (most probably Aaron Barting), c. 1775. H. 30 mm. PG

136 Pendant scent bottle. Coral with gold mounts and chain. Hinged lid in the shape of a female face. Body of flacon with carved scrolls. European, 18/19th Ct. H. 41 mm. PG

137 Enamel scent bottle with representation of a courting couple in a river landscape. Gilt-bronze mounts. England, 1753/56. H. 90 mm. The stopper is a later addition. C. Schwarzkopf.

138 Scent bottle of a flattened pear-shape. Blue glass overlaid with superb gold cagework, set with diamonds, a pearl and garnets. In front an inserted watch and on the reverse a compass; the stopper, formed by the watch key, crowned by a pearl surrounded by garnets. The base, fringed by diamonds, contains a lidded box with mirror for holding "mouches" (patches). The cagework consists of floral scrolls and animal motifs. England, workshop of James Cox, London, 1775–1785. H. 135 mm. Christie, Manson & Wood Ltd. ▷

139 Scent bottle of cobalt-blue glass, shape and mount as above. England, c. 1780. H. 70 mm. P. London

140 Scent bottle. Clear glass with gold mount and enamel medallion. England, c. 1780. H. 70 mm. P. London

139 △   140 ▽

141 △   144 ▽   142 △   145 ▽   143 △   146 ▽

141 Scent bottle. Rock crystal painted with enamel colours with a bird motif pewter mount. South Germany, c. 1700. H. 77 mm. C. Schwarzkopf.

142 Scent bottle. Thick-walled glass with elegant gold mount shaped in imitation of a wickerwork flask. Switzerland, 2nd h. 18th Ct. H. 110 mm. PG

143 Scent bottle. Agate, flat base of gold with engraved rosette. Stopper made of darker agate in the form of a female head, with both the neck and head set with cut gems. Origin? Early 19th Ct. H. 50 mm. PG

144 Repoussé silver scent bottle with shell decoration, with flat circular foot and suspensory ring. Germany, Augsburg 1725. H. 84 mm. P. London

145 Scent bottle with relief bust of a lady with Empire headress and diadem. Cast iron, with brass screw-top. Germany, Berlin, early 19th Ct. H. 97 mm. C. Schwarzkopf.

146 Scent bottle. Hinged lid over ground glass stopper. At the four sides and on the lid glass-covered ivory tablets with painted views of Paris. Gold, base carnelian. France, after 1836. H. 43 mm. P. London.

147 Miniature scent bottle. Back and front held together by a band of filigree. Front with four precious stones. Lapis Lazuli, opal, vermeil (garnet), and emerald, the first letters of which form the word "Love". On the reverse a medallion with plaited real hair. England, early 19th Ct. H. 45 mm. CG

148 Scent bottle. Bloodstone, with elaborate silver cagework and set with rubies and sapphires. France, 2nd h. 19th Ct. H. 145 mm. P. Munich.

149 Bridal scent bottle. Silver, decorated with flowers and set with tear-shaped almandines. Bohemia, 2nd h. 19th Ct. H. 100 mm. C. Schwarzkopf.

150 Silver scent bottle with highly polished surface and a bullfinch painted in subtle enamel colours. Original padded leather etui with wing-like hinged lids. England, etui by Mappin & Webb, London; flacon Birmingham, H. & H. 1899. H. 110 mm. P. London.

147 △

149 ▽　　148 △

150 ▽

◁◁ 151 Conical silver scent bottle with floral decoration, screw-top. England, W. Comyns, 1890/91. H. 245 mm. C. Schwarzkopf.

◁ 152 Cylindrical scent bottle case decorated with stylised mistletoe in relief. Brass, holding a glass flacon. France c. 1900. H. 60 mm. P. Hamburg.

153 Scent bottle with silver overlay. Germany, c. 1925/30 (f. l. to r.) Light blue porcelain with birds of paradise and inscription "F. M. B.", dated 25. 1. 30. H. 57 mm. – Red porcelain with a bird of prey, cork stopper with metal crown. H. 60 mm. – Dark blue glass with fan-like decoration. Screw top with tassel. H. 57 mm. – Dark blue porcelain with stylised flower. Mark on base "XF 5.1". H. 54 mm. – Blue porcelain. Globular screw top. H. 62 mm. P. Hamburg.　　▽

154 Splendid perfume fountain for a princely table, made from one half of husked "sea coconut" (coco-de-mer), the fruit of a palm tree native to the Seychelles. The mounting in silver-gilt is lavishly decorated in the Mannerist style. The actual perfume container rests on a flat silver dish, supported by a baluster-like column which displays masks and is connected with the lid by two finely worked buckles. The crowning figure is obviously different in style and was added much later (19th Ct?). It has been removed recently. Germany, c. 1580. H. 410 mm. BM

155 △   156 △   158 ▽   157 △

155 Scent bottle made from a carved tropical nut, with silver mount. England, late 16th Ct. H. 84 mm. C. Schwarzkopf.

156 Pendant scent bottle made from a pine cone. Gold mount, decorated with white and translucent red enamel colours (the enamelling is largely rubbed off). Spain, Treasury of the Cathedral of the Virgin of the Pillar, Saragossa (certainly a pilgrim's gift to the shrine) c. 1600. H. 80 mm. V. & A.

157 Scent bottle made of hartshorn with silver mounts. In front the carved figure of a girl with wickerwork flask and a drinking cup. On the reverse two drunken female figures with a cornucopia screw cap. Chain modern. Germany, 17/18th Ct. H. 60 mm. PG

◁ 158 Left: Scent bottle, made of thick brown leather. Glass stopper beneath hinged brass lid; chain and finger ring. England, late 19th Ct. H. 40 mm. – Right: scent bottle made of dark-brown hardwood, with manufactured silver mount. Glass stopper beneath hinged lid; silver chain with suspensory ring. South America?, late 19th Ct. H. 75 mm. CG

159 Scent bottle made from a carved nut, richly ornamented. Silver stopper with chain attached to lateral loops. Germany, 17th Ct. D. 47 mm. C. Schwarzkopf.

160 Scent bottle made from root of walnut. Silver mount and silver stopper. On the underside of the small foot the initials "F. G. D. Q.". Germany or Holland, 1758. H. 85 mm. PG   ▷

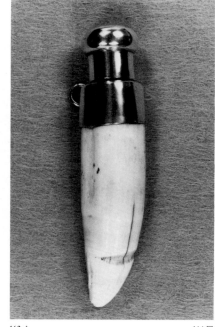

161 Scent bottle in the form of a bunch of grapes. Ivory, silver top. Germany, 1st h. 18th Ct. H. 70 mm. C. Schwarzkopf.

162 Scent bottle made from a tiger's fang; glass stopper. England 19/20th Ct. H. 75 mm. CG

163 Scent bottle in the form of two fighting cherubs, on a turned circular foot. Ivory. Germany, 17th Ct. H. 70 mm. KGMB

164 Scent bottle, with carved intertwined foliage motifs on a female bust. Ivory with bronze mount. Germany, 17th Ct. H. 68 mm. KGMB

165 Scent bottle with rich engraved embellishments. In front representation of a cavalier; on the reverse a lady, both surrounded by stylised foliage. Hartshorn with bronze screw-top. Probably a wedding gift. Germany 17th Ct. H. 33 mm. KGMB

161 △   163 ▽   162 △   164 ▽   165 ▽

167 Scent bottle. Amber with gold mounts. The lid secured by small chains. On underside of foot are engraved the names of Friedrich and Carl von Hesse and the date 1759. Germany 1759. R

◁ 166 Scent bottle. Amber with silver mounts and set with garnets. Danzig(?), perhaps mounted in Russia, c. 1600. H. 80 mm. Hermitage Museum, Leningrad.

168 △   169 △   170 △   171 ▽

168   Scent bottle. Tortoiseshell with gold piqué work consisting of stylised flowers and
foliage. Gilt hinged lid. England mid 19th Ct.
D. 33 mm. PG

169   Scent bottle of lozenge shape. Silver
with engraved panels of mother-of-pearl. In
front a boy with birdcage beneath a weeping
willow, in addition scrolls and foliage motifs.
Silver stopper with suspensory loop. Germany, 17/18th Ct. P. Frankfurt.

170   Flacon. Constructed from a pair of
shells held together by brass mountings. Cork
stopper and suspensory ring with chain. England, late 19th Ct. H. 75 mm. P. London

171   Bellows for perfumed powder. Mother-
of-pearl, gold and thin leather. France,
Paris, 18th Ct. D. 75 mm. – The powder
was squirted through a fine hole disguised
as a flower in the centre of the hinged lid.
C. Schwarzkopf.   ▷

Enamel flacons

172 Four-sided columnar pendant scent bottle with dome shaped lid and chain. The lid with suspensory ring is fastened by a separate delicate chain. Silver-gilt and with black enamel on a white background. Spain or France, 17/18th Ct. P. Frankfurt.

173 Heart-shaped enamel scent bottle with silver mount and push-on stopper which is fastened by a small chain. Decoration of individual flowers, a fruit bowl and foliage. Holland (?) mid 17th Ct. H. 50 mm. P. Hastings.

174 Enamel flacon in the form of an articulated fish. Italy, Venice, 17th Ct. L. 140 mm. KHMW

172 △

173 △

174 ▽

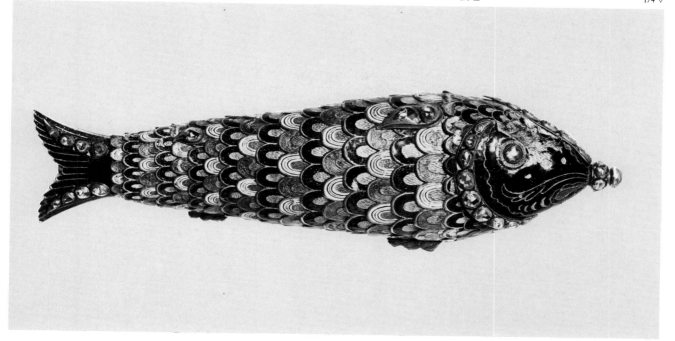

175 △   177 ▽   176 △   178 ▽

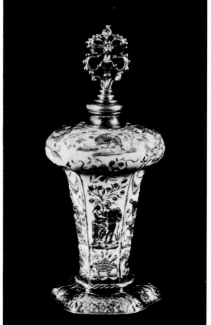

175 Enamel flacon in the form of a boy gardener. Metal mounted and metal stopper. England, Staffordshire, 3rd qu. 18th Ct. H. 70 mm. Sotheby & Co. – This figure is clearly modelled on a Chelsea porcelain scent bottle (Ill. 235) which has, however, a bunch of flowers forming the stopper.

176 Pear-shaped flattened enamel scent bottle. Painted with flowers and a shepherdess in a landscape with ruins. England, Birmingham, c. 1760. H. 90 mm. V. & A. – In shape and decoration this bottle differs from all other English enamel flacons attributed to Staffordshire.

177 Urn-shaped enamel flacon with four representations of figures in applied gold-relief and coloured flowers. Mounts on foot and top silver-gilt. Germany, Augsburg or Berlin (Fromery?), mid 18th Ct. H. 95 mm. P. Munich.

178 Enamel scent bottle with silver-gilt mount. In front an idyllic painting in the style of Watteau, depicting a group of anglers. Also gilded flowers in relief. England, South Staffordshire, 18th Ct. H. 81 mm. PG.

Facing page:
179 Enamel scent bottle with painted flower decorations. Detachable circular foot; silver-mounted and set with garnets along the edges; Silver screw stopper. Holland or Germany, 2nd h. 17th Ct. H. 60 mm. P. London.

180 Enamel flacon in the shape of a pilgrim's flask. Gold with a flower decorated screw lid. Neck painted with hunting scenes and the main body with representations from classical mythology. France, 3rd qu. 17th Ct. H. 38 mm. PG

181 Silver-mounted enamel flacon. Lid with suspensory ring. On either side representations of courting couples in a landscape: a youthful one in front and an aged one on the reverse. Germany, 18th Ct. H. 76 mm. PG

179 △

180 ▽

182 Gold and enamel automata flacon, a rare combination of scent bottle and a musical clock. Behind the wing doors one observes a singing young couple accompanied by a lady on a cymbal. The flacon, closed by an acorn-shaped stopper is in the upper part of this luxurious object. An enamelled miniature portrait of a lady is fringed with pearls. Switzerland, Genève, 1st qu. 19th Ct. H. 21 cm. Sotheby & Co.

Facing page:
183 Three enamel flacons, the first and third with flower decorations, the second with a harbour scene and elegant scrolls. All England (the left hand one perhaps London, c. 1760) Staffordshire, 3rd qu. 18th Ct. (f. l. to r.) H. 60 mm, 65 mm, 65 mm. V. & A.

184 Left enamel flacon as in Ill. 178 but with light blue ground and a trellis-work pattern; in the reserve a landscape painting. England, Staffordshire (perhaps Wednesbury), 3rd qu. 18th Ct. H. 98 mm. – Centre: Enamel flacon in the shape of billing doves, the white ribbon is tied in a lover's knot and inscribed "Nos amoureux coeurs s'éloignent de peurs". England, Staffordshire, 3rd qu. 18th Ct. H. 85 mm. – Right: Enamel flacon with metal mounts and stopper in Rococo style. Surrounded by scrolls the portrait of Lady Fenhoulet based on a painting by Joshua Reynolds. England, Staffordshire, 3rd qu. 18th Ct. H. 127 mm. Sotheby & Co.

183 △

184 ▽

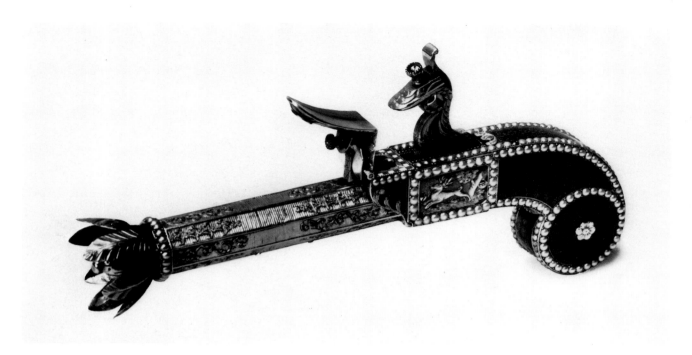

185 Perfume spray in the form of a flintlock pistol. The handle is enamelled and set with pearls as is the mouth of the engraved golden barrel. In the centre part an enamel panel with hunting scene. When the trigger is pulled gilded flower petals protrude from the barrel and release a squirt of perfume. Switzerland, early 19th Ct. L. 108 mm. Sotheby & Co.

◁◁ 186 Scent bottle. Whitish-grey and gold enamel painting on a dark brown background. France, c. 1870. H. 57 mm. – On the reverse two birds in a rose bush, on the lid a garland with a butterfly. C. Schwarzkopf.

◁ 187 Left: Enamel flacon with copper mount. A shepherdess with lamb collecting herbs. France, 2nd h. 19th Ct. H. 50 mm. – Right: Enamel flacon with gold mount. A girl with child picking flowers, on the lid a music score with torch, trumpet and drum; gold-mounted ivory stopper. France, 2nd h. 19th Ct. H. 77 mm. C. Schwarzkopf.

188 △

189 ▽

188 Flacon in the form of a pocket watch. Salt-glazed stoneware. This flacon was most probably used as a smelling bottle and had a cork stopper. England, Fulham?, after 1845. H. 82 mm. PG

189 Flacon. Stoneware richly decorated in relief (beige and green on a brown ground) with ferns surrounded horseshoe fashion by rows of pearls. Gold mount with miniature lock on the hinged lid. England, Doulton (Lambeth), c. 1890. H. 69 mm. PG

190 Porcelain scent bottle in the form of a gourd. Dark lilac ground, painting with a rural scene and on the reverse a delicate harbour scene. Unusual is the presence of a second painted reserve on the bulging neck of this bottle. Silver mount and stopper. Germany, Meissen, c. 1740. H. 100 mm. V. & A.

191, 192   Porcelain scent bottles in the shape of pilgrim's flasks, painted in polychrome on a white ground with chinoiseries. With silver or silver-gilt mounts. Germany, Meissen c. 1725. H. 90 mm. RA

◁◁ 193   Vase-like flacon, gourd-shaped. White porcelain with "red dragon" motif and flower decoration in the Kakiemon style (iron red and gold colours). Germany, Meissen, 1730–1740. H. 69 mm. BNM

◁ 194   Typical Rococo flacon. White porcelain painted with "Goldchinesen" (gold Chinamen). The silver stopper in the form of a sea creature. Gold painting most probably Augsburg "Hausmalerei". Germany, Meissen, c. 1730. H. 135 mm. KGMK

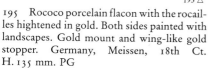

195 △   196 △   198 ▽   197 △   199 ▽

195   Rococo porcelain flacon with the rocailles hightened in gold. Both sides painted with landscapes. Gold mount and wing-like gold stopper. Germany, Meissen, 18th Ct. H. 135 mm. PG

196   Porcelain flacon of Rococo form. White porcelain with representation of a traveller. Gilt mounts. Germany, Frankenthal, 1770. H. 80 mm. MKG

197   Flacon in the form of a laterally flattened urn tapering towards both ends. White porcelain surface with rocailles heightened by gilding. Painted on both sides with flower sprays. Gold mounts along the rim with a row of stiff leaves. Porcelain stopper in the form of a bird. England, Chelsea ("Gold Anchor" period) c. 1760. H. 89 mm. PG

198   Scent bottle with flower painting. Rococo gilt copper mounts. England "Girl in a Swing", 1749–1754. H. 89 mm. MKG

199   Porcelain with purple-red painted scenes. Gilt copper mount. Denmark, Copenhagen, c. 1780. H. 92 mm. MKG

200 Porcelain flacon with "Osier" relief and flower painting. Stopper crowned by an enamelled flower bouquet held by a chain. Golden blue mark "N:e". France, c. 1760/70. H. 80 mm. MKG/CB

201, 202 Two-lidded porcelain scent bottles. Decorated in gold with scrolls and stylised foliage and painted in "schwarzlot" between vertical ridges with cherubs. Austria, Vienna, Du Paquier, 1718–1744. H. 150 mm. MAKW

200

201

202 △

203 △   205 ▽

204 △   206 ▽

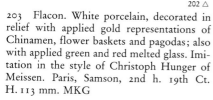

203 Flacon. White porcelain, decorated in relief with applied gold representations of Chinamen, flower baskets and pagodas; also with applied green and red melted glass. Imitation in the style of Christoph Hunger of Meissen. Paris, Samson, 2nd h. 19th Ct. H. 113 mm. MKG

204 Porcelain scent bottle with painting in iron-red, purple, green and gold. Gold screw top with chain. Austria, Vienna, Du Paquier, c. 1735. MKG/SB

205, 206 Porcelain flacon with copper mount, press mark "1/77". Along the narrow surfaces is a trellis pattern in gold. Painting in purple, blue, green, yellow and black. On the reverse the monogram FR (= Friedericus Rex) beneath a crown and the inscription "VIVAT Friedericus Maximus". Germany, Berlin, Wegely, c. 1755. H. 22 mm. MKG/CB

207 △ 208 ▽

Facing page:

207 Heart-shaped scent bottle. On a grey-ish-white ground a painting of a girl with a bird besides a splendid vase with flowers. The stopper (missing here) takes the form of a flame, continued from the neck of the flacon. Italy, Le Nove, c. 1810. H. 60 mm. V. & A.

208 Porcelain scent bottle with representation in relief of Amor and nymph. Silver mounts. Italy, Doccia, Conte Ginori, c. 1745. H. 95 mm. – On the reverse the reclining nymph expecting Amor approaching with bow and a wreath of flowers. The stopper is embellished by two male relief portraits. The original leather etui is padded with blue silk. MKG

209 Flacon with two portraits of a black-haired woman. Porcelain, silver-gilt mounts. Italy, Doccia, 3rd q. 18th Ct. H. 60 mm. C. Schwarzkopf.

210 △   211 ▽   212 ▽

210 Three flacons in the form of fruits. Porcelain with gilt copper mounts, without marks. Germany, Fürstenberg c. 1760/70. Left: Yellow and red painted pear with leaf, a brown twig forming the stopper. H. 90 mm. MKG. Centre: Pear, painted red on yellow ground. Gilt stopper shaped as a leaf. H. 64 mm. MKG. Right: a fig split open exposing red fruit flesh. Stopper in the form of twig cum leaf. H. 93 mm. MKG/CB

211 Flacon in the form of a lady holding a small dog. The dog's head forming the stopper. Porcelain with gilt copper mount. Germany, Fürstenberg, modelled by Simon Feilner (?), c. 1765. H. 109 mm. MKG/CB

212 Flacon in the form of a bird with black-brown plumage. The bird's head forms the stopper. Porcelain. Gilt copper mount. Germany, Fürstenberg, c. 1765/70. H. 65 mm. MKG

◁◁ 213 Flacon in the form of Harlequin, wearing a chequered garment. His head, with white colour, forms the stopper. Porcelain. Germany, Gera, c. 1780/90. MKG

◁ 214 Flacon in the form of Harlequin. Porcelain with gilt copper mount. Germany, Meissen. Crossed-sword mark, c. 1750/60. H. 82 mm – Harlequin in his colourful (yellow, green and violet) attire leans against a gold-embellished pillar which is crowned by a pine cone forming the stopper. Whereas his right hand is raised for a salute the left holds, concealed by his head, a golden flap. MKG/CB

◁ 215 Two double flacons: "Provender for the monastery". Porcelain with gilt copper mounts. Germany, Meissen, c. 1770. Left: A monk carries eggs and a goose with black-violet plumage in a white basket. Over his shoulder a girl concealed in a white sheaf of wheat (2nd stopper missing). H. 80 mm. MKG. Right: The monk carries a white goose. The girl is hidden in a yellow sheaf, the second stopper (on the sheaf) is in the form of a bee. H. 86 mm. MKG/CB

216 Pierrot flacon. Porcelain with silver-gilt mounts. Germany (Thuringia), Kloster Veilsdorf(?), c. 1770. H. 116 mm. – His white garment is fastened by large violet buttons. In his right hand he holds a mask. The head with yellow hat forms the stopper. Beneath the grass green pedestal is a small smelling box with pierced and engraved grille, the porcelain lid is painted with a bird and scroll. MKG/CB

▷

217 Flacon. Hercules and Omphale seated on a throne. Porcelain with silver mount. Germany (Thuringia), Kloster Veilsdorf, c. 1770/80. H. 83 mm. – Omphale, clad in a white cloth rests on Hercules's lap; he has raised his left hand to draw the curtain. The baldachin is crowned by the stopper. MGK

▷ ▷

218 Flacon. Itinerant tradesman with walking stick and wide-brimmed hat. The wicker basket on his back forms the flacon. Porcelain with gilt copper mount, not marked. Germany (Thuringia), Kloster Veilsdorf (probably modelled by Wenzel Neu) c. 1765. H. 105 mm. MKG/CB

▷

219 Flacon taking the form of a man riding a sheep. Porcelain with gold mount: not marked. Germany, Kelsterbach, c. 1761/65. H. 59 mm. – A man with striped shirt, red-spotted white breeches, violet shoes and a green hat sits astride a sheep. The upper part of the hat contains the gold stopper. MKG/CB

▷ ▷

220 Four flacons in the form of goatherds. Porcelain (f. l. to r.): Germany, Kelsterbach, probably modelled by Carl Vogelmann, c. 1761/65. H. 77 mm. MKG/CB. – Plain white porcelain with silver mounts. Kelsterbach, c. 1765. H. 75 mm. MKG. – With silver mounts. Under foot with engraved flower motif, England, Chelsea, c. 1760. H. 78 mm. MKG. – Without stopper. Germany, Gera, c. 1780/90. H. 62 mm. MKG

◁ 221 Flacon in the form of a goatherd with black hat leaning against a tree trunk and holding a goat by its horns. Porcelain. Gilt-bronze mount and stopper. Germany (Thuringia), Kloster Veilsdorf (modelled by Fr. Wilhelm Eugen Doll, 1750–1816), c. 1767/70. H. 109 mm. C. Schwarzkopf.

Facing page:
222 Flacon in the form of a huntsman with gun and bag. Porcelain with gold mount. Germany, Ludwigsburg, c. 1760. H. 77 mm. – The head functions as stopper; on underside of base painted flowers. C. Schwarzkopf.

223 Flacon in the form of a goatherd. The stopper in the shape of a butterfly; copper mounts and small chain. Germany, Kelsterbach, c. 1765. H. 80 mm. C. Schwarzkopf.

224 Double flacon in the shape of an urn with a resting greyhound. Porcelain with gold mounts. Base with gold hinged lid covering a bonbonnière or box for patches which is painted inside with flower sprays. The dog's head (a replacement here) forms the stopper for the second flacon. In other pieces of the same model the main stopper on the urn takes the form of a bird! England, "Girl in a Swing", 1749–1754. H. 72 mm. PG

222 △

223 ▽

225 △

226 ▽

Facing page:

225 Flacon in the form of a pear. Porcelain. Germany, Fürstenberg 2nd h. 18th Ct. H. 63 mm. C. Schwarzkopf.

226 Rococo flacon. Porcelain with flower spray and gilt copper mounts. Stopper, connected to the rim by a small chain, taking the form of a cockerel. Origin?, c. 1760. H. 104 mm. C. Schwarzkopf.

227 Flacon with representation of two scenes from Greek mythology in white relief on blue jasper-ware. Copper screw lid. England, (Wedgwood) Etruria, c. 1790. H. 82 mm. C. Schwarzkopf.

228 Flacon in the form of a hunchbacked dwarf riding on a turtle. Porcelain. Italy, Capodimonte (probably modelled by Giuseppe Gricci), c. 1750/55. H. 82 mm. – The dwarf with his face partly masked shows his tongue, a purple hairbag protrudes from beneath the white hat; in the top of this is the opening of the flacon (stopper missing). MKG/CB ▷

229 Left: Double flacon in the form of a parrot and a black spotted Cochinchina cock. On the underside painted flowers. Porcelain. England "Girl in a Swing", 1749–1754. H. 72 mm. – Centre: Flacon in the form of a nesting duck with four ducklings. Under the base painted flowers. Porcelain. England, Chelsea (red anchor period) c. 1755. H. 89 mm. – Right: Double flacon in the form of billing doves. Underside of base a painted flower spray surrounded by leaves. Porcelain. England, "Girl in a Swing", 1749–1754. H. 55 mm. MKG/CB

230 Left: Flacon in the form of Cupid and an ass. The ribbon is inscribed "TELS SONT MES DISCIPLES". On underside of base green framed flowers painted in gold. Porcelain. England, Chelsea (gold anchor period), c. 1760. H. 92 mm. – Centre: Flacon with two masked cherubs and dog and the inscription "CONTENTONS NOS DESIRS". Underside of base a black network on a green ground. Porcelain. England, "Girl in a Swing", 1749–1754. H. 75 mm. – Right: Flacon in the form of a drunken Cupid. The shoulder-ribbon says "IL EST VAINCU". Underside of base blue-framed flower painting. Porcelain. England, Chelsea (gold anchor period), c. 1760. H. 82 mm. MKG/CB

231 Flacon in the form of a broad-shouldered urn with four sided neck, raised foliage decoration and ram's heads on either side. England, "Girl in a Swing" 1749–1754. H. 70 mm. V. & A.

232 Underside of the Shakespeare flacon (Ill. 233).

233 Flacon in imitation of the Shakespeare monument by Peter Scheemakers (1691–1781) in Westminster Abbey (1740). Porcelain. England, "Girl in a Swing", 1749–1754. BM

231 △

232 ▽

234 △   236 ▽   235 △   237 ▽

234   Double flacon in the form of a clergyman. Underside of base flower painting. Porcelain. Gilt copper mounts. England, Chelsea (red anchor period) c. 1760. H. 87 mm. MKG

235   Flacon in the form of a boy as gardener (see also Ill. 175). Porcelain with metal stopper shaped as a bouquet. England, "Girl in a Swing" 1749–1754. H. 93 mm. V. & A.

236   Flacon in the form of a little drummer. Porcelain with metal mount and porcelain, stopper taking the shape of a butterfly. England, "Girl in a Swing", 1749–1754. H. 72 mm. V. & A.

237   Flacon formed as a fountain. Underside the base a bough of roses surrounded by leaves. Gilt copper mount. England, "Girl in a Swing", 1749–1754. H. 78 mm. MKG

Facing page:
238   Flacon in the form of a girl picking berries. Inscription on the gold rimmed base "A MON AMOUR". Underside of base with a single painted rose. Porcelain. England "Girl in a Swing", 1749–1754. H. 78 mm. Sotheby & Co.

239   Flacon representing Venus with a clock supported by Cupid. England, "Girl in a Swing", 1749–1754. H. 80 mm. Sotheby & Co.

240   Flacon in the form of a lady playing the hurdy-gurdy. The gold mounted base on the underside with a spray of flowers. England, "Girl in a Swing", 1749–1754. H. 78 mm. Sotheby & Co.

241   Flacon in the form of a flower bouquet of forget-me-nots, carnations and orange blossoms. Porcelain. Gold mount. England, "Girl in a Swing", 1749–1754. H. 76 mm. MKG

242   Three flacons in the form of bird catcher and flute player. Porcelain. Gilt copper mounts. England, Chelsea (gold anchor period) c. 1760. H. (f. l. t. r.) 89 mm, 67 mm, 85 mm. MKG/CB

164

238 △   241 ▽   239 △   240 △   242 ▽

243 Flacon representing a "Scène galante". The stopper is crowned by two roses. Porcelain. Gold mount. England, "Girl in a Swing", 1749–1754. H. 110 mm. MKG

244 Flacon in the form of a flower girl. Porcelain. Gilt copper mount. England, "Girl in a Swing", 1749–1754. H. 40 mm. The girl with a rose-decorated dress underneath a white apron holds a dove in her hands. At her feet sits a Dalmation dog. The stopper on top of the yellow basket on her back is crowned by two porcelain roses. Underside of base black twigs on a light-green ground. MKG ▽

245 △

246 △

248 ▽

247 △

249 ▽

245 Flacon in the form of a frightened Harlequin with cat and mouse. Porcelain. Origin? (most probably German), c. 1760. H. 60 mm. MKG/CB

246 Flacon representing a rural "Scène galante". Porcelain. Gilt copper mounts and stopper. Germany(?) 19th Ct. H. 99 mm. C. Schwarzkopf.

247 Flacon representing a drinking Harlequin. Porcelain. Origin?, c. 1760. H. 110 mm. Harlequin is pulled by his hair by a monkey. The hat, put on a tree trunk, forms the stopper, which is crowned by a crowing cock. MKG/CB

248 Flacon representing a Chinese "scène de famille" with a breast-feeding mother. Underside of base a single painted rose framed by leaves. Porcelain. Gold mount. England, "Girl in a Swing". 1749–1754. H. 86 mm. MKG/CB

249 Flacon representing a Far Eastern "scène galante". Underside of base as above. Gold mount. England, "Girl in a Swing", 1749–1754. H. 96 mm. MKG/CB

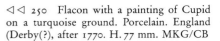

◁◁ 250 Flacon with a painting of Cupid on a turquoise ground. Porcelain. England (Derby(?), after 1770. H. 77 mm. MKG/CB

◁ 251 Flat octangular flacon. Blue jasper-ware, probably modelled by John Loche. Classical inspired figures surrounded by a band of leaves (in relief). Silver screw lid above stopper. England (Wedgwood), Etruria, c. 1790. H. 55 mm. V. & A. – In the same museum there is a flacon of identical shape but with a portrait of the Prince of Wales (later King George IV).

◁◁ 252 Flacon. Green jasper-ware with white relief decoration. Copper mount. On the reverse a female Genius at sacrifice. England (Wedgwood), Etruria, c. 1790. H. 70 mm. MKG

◁ 253 Flat elliptical flacon. On one side a motif in relief after a design by Lady Templeton, on the other a mother with child. Dipped blue jaster ware in imitation of Wedgwood. England, Staffordshire (probably John Turner), late 18th Ct. H. 85 mm. V. & A.

254 Miniature flacons. The left one in the form of a lamp, decorated in green, pink and gold, brass mount. H. 30 mm. The middle one shell-shaped, decorated with gold on a blue ground below and on a yellow ground above, and the inscription "Souvenir", brass lid. H. 30 mm. – The right one is oval-shaped with blunt marginal notches; decorated with gold and intense blue and with red dots on the free surfaces. Silver lid. All: France, 19th Ct. CG ▷

255, 256 Two bulging flacons. Painted porcelain. Gilt copper mounts. Germany, Meissen (Marcolini mark) 1800. H. 135 mm. C. Schwarzkopf.

257 Flacon with heads in relief and cherub-scenes painted in purple camaieu. Porcelain, gilt bronze mount. Unmarked. Germany, modelled after a Meissen piece, 1770/80. H. 81 mm. C. Schwarzkopf.

255 ▽

256 ▽

257 ▽

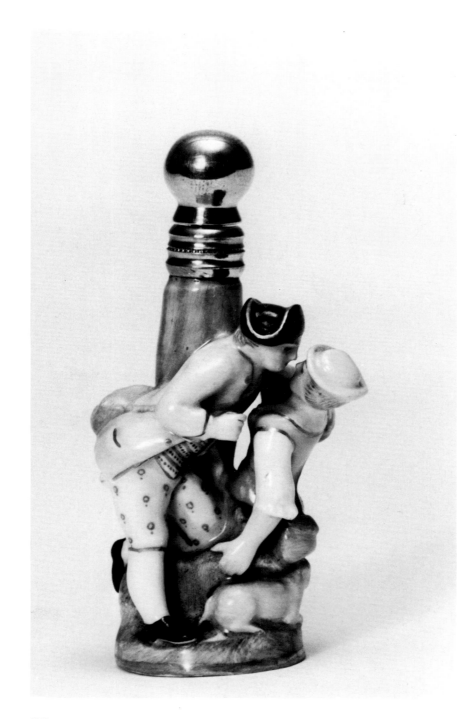

259 △   260 ▽

Facing page:

258 Flacon representing a "scène galante". Gilt brass stopper. Germany, Meissen (sword mark), after 1860. C. Schwarzkopf.

259 Flacon in the form of a young lady with flower basket. Porcelain. France, Fontainbleau, Jacob Petit, c. 1840. H. 170 mm. – She is dressed in a green bodice and a gold dotted white skirt. The stopper is hidden in her black hat. C. Schwarzkopf.

260 Flacon "Provender for the monastery", Porcelain, Thuringia, Ohrdruff, Christian Friedrich Kling, c. 1850/60. H. 78 mm. The monk carries a goose, his purse and a girl hidden in a sheaf of wheat (see also Ill. 215). C. Schwarzkopf.

261 △   263 ▽   262 △   264 ▽

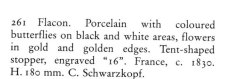

261 Flacon. Porcelain with coloured butterflies on black and white areas, flowers in gold and golden edges. Tent-shaped stopper, engraved "16". France, c. 1830. H. 180 mm. C. Schwarzkopf.

262 Flacon. Porcelain with painted flowers and gilding. Germany, Thuringia, Schlaggenwald. Mid 19th Ct. H. 110 mm. MKG

263 Flacon. Porcelain, reminiscent of pressed glass. With delicate gold edges. Germany, Meissen (sword marks), c. 1840. H. 130 mm. C. Schwarzkopf.

264 Flacon. Porcelain with stylised gold painting. Germany, Meissen (sword mark), c. 1840. H. 130 mm. C. Schwarzkopf.

265

266

267

265 Flacon. Painted and gilded porcelain, with two female portraits in "pâte-sur-pâte". Germany, Meissen, before 1897. H. 120 mm. MKG

266 Flacon. Porcelain, underglaze painted with everlasting flowers. Gold hinged lid. Netherlands, late 19th Ct. H. 85 mm. C. Schwarzkopf.

267 Flacon. Porcelain with painted representation of Wartburg castle, Germany, Thuringia, c. 1860. C. Schwarzkopf.

To page 173:
268 Egg-shaped flacon. Porcelain, painted with a rickshaw. Brass mount and chain. England, mid 19th Ct. H. 65 mm. C. Schwarzkopf.

269 Flacons in imitation of bird eggs. Porcelain. England (Macintyre & Co., Washington China Works), Burslem. Silver mounts. f. l. to r.: Birmingham (B. G. W.), 1889; Birmingham (C. S. & R. S.), 1891; London (S. Mordan), 1886. H. 60 mm. CG

270, 271 Two egg-shaped flacons. Porcelain. Cork stoppers with gilt bronze. Unmarked. Germany, Königliche Porzellanmanufaktur Berlin. 2nd h. 19th Ct. – 270: on

the reverse in italics "Der Osterhase" (Easter bunny). H. 62 mm. – 271: Two cherubs painted orange-red H. 80 mm. C. Schwarzkopf.

272 Flacon. Porcelain. With painted portrait of Queen Mary Antoinette within rocailles in relief. Brass lid with chain and suspensory ring. England, c. 1870. H. 56 mm. C. Schwarzkopf.

273 Flacon with representation of a girl in enamel paint. Gilt copper mount. England late 18th Ct. H. 63 mm. C. Schwarzkopf.

◁ 268

269 △

270 △

272 ▽

271 △

273 ▽

274 Kitsch flacon. Souvenir from Bognor Regis. On the reverse at the base the impressed inscription "GERMANY". Germany, late 19th Ct. H. 93 mm. P. London.

275 "Pisseuse à parfum". Perfum sprinkler in the form of a girl performing an intimate function. This charmingly frivolous piece has a similar counterpart in the Musée d'Art et d'Histoire in Grasse. The latter has no chamber pot, but it still has the original rubber tube. The figure was filled with toilet water or cheap perfume. When pressed the ball released a scented jet from a small opening between the delicately bared thighs of the young lady. Unglazed porcelain. Late 19th century. H. 85 mm. German experts maintain that France, French experts that Germany is the country of manufacture. Neither wishes to lay claim to it. P. London.

Glass flacons

278 Flacon in form of a sea creature. Opaque white glass with coloured glass streaks, attached glass prunts and combed margin. Silver stopper. Venice, 17th Ct. H. 90 mm. P. London.

279 Flacon in the form of a shell. Mould-blown amber coloured glass with white opaque glass threads. Pewter mount and stopper. France, Orleans, c. 1675. H. 70 mm. P. London.

280 Flacon. Opaque white glass with blue glass threads. Pewter mounts. The flacon on the right takes the form of a fica. Venice, 18th Ct. H (r) 110 mm, (l) 60 mm. C. Schwarzkopf.

278 △

279 △

280 ▽

To page 174:
276 Flacon in the form of a stylised female head. Stopper on underside. White glazed porcelain. Impressed mark. "Fochtenberger ca 150 ccm". Germany, Thomas, Bavaria, c. 1930. H. 130 mm. C. Schwarzkopf.

277 Atomiser. Porcelain body with fine vertical fluting, sea-green. Nickelled metal mount. Rubber bulb concealed in tassel. Germany, Nymphenburg, designer Prof. W. v. Wersin, 1938. H. 110 mm. P. London

281 Flacons. Glass cut all over with shallow facets and with gilt and enamel painting. Gold repoussé screw caps. England, 1775/80. H. 84 mm. The reverse of the blue flacon is painted with a flowering tree with birds and butterflies. MKG.

282 Left: Flacon cum box. Clear glass with inset silver box for patches or rouge. The engraved hinged lid is embellished with a "gem" of cobalt glass. – Right: Flacon. Cobalt glass with inset silver-mounted enamel panel. England, Birmingham, c. 1785. H. 115 mm. P. London.

▷

Facing page:
283 Flacon. Facet-cut ruby red glass. Silver-gilt mount and screw cap. Germany early 18th Ct. H. 80 mm. C. Schwarzkopf.

284 Toilet water flask in the form of a dove. Fill hole with glass stopper on back; spray hole in beak. Cobalt blue glass with gilt decoration. Turkey 1st h. 19th Ct. H. 200 mm. C. Schwarzkopf.

285 Urn-shaped flacon. Lithyalin glass. Gold mount set with turquoise. Bohemia, c. 1830. H. 57 mm. C. Schwarzkopf.

286 Early throw-away scent bottles for rose or lavender oil. Glass. Usually coarsely cut and/or decorated in gilt or enamel paints in a manner reminiscent of folk art; occasionally set with glass "gems". Bohemia (Isergebirge) and perhaps later also Germany. 1st h. 19th Ct. L. 170–185 mm. P. London.

283 △

284 △

285 ▽

286 ▽

287 Left: Broad-shouldered toilet water flask. Clear glass, facet-cut and gold painted in the style of the late Rococo. Ground glass stopper. Flasks of this type often occur in pairs or sets in travel toilet cases or in needle-work boxes of this period. Germany or Bohemia, late 18th Ct. H. 80 mm. – Right: Atomiser with plunger mechanism. Partly matted glass, decorated in high relief with female dancers in diaphanous garments. Gilt bronze mount. France, René Lalique, early 20th Ct. H. 155 mm. P. London.

288 △

289 ▽

288 Flacons in the form of negroid heads. Mould-blown whitish-blue opaque glass, with facial features painted. Silver (l) and pewter (r) mount. Venice (in some literature attributed to Orleans). 17th Ct. H. 65 mm. P. London – Similar but equally rare are flacons of this shape in black glass.

289 Selection of medicine vials, bottles and jars which were also used for holding aromatic substances and on the shape of which some early scent bottles were based. Clear glass, brown glass or green "Waldglas". The two long cylindrical vials are so-called "Rosolen-flaschen" in which eau de cologne, which was originally sold as a medicine, was traded (fig. 22). The flared neck of these vials facilitated closure by parchment and/or cork with seal-ing wax. Germany and England, early 16th to 18th Ct. H. 20–40 mm (the "Rosolen" 240 mm). P. London.

290 Flacon of flattened pear-shape with slightly flaring mouth and foot. Thick green glass with combed opaque white trail-work and applied pincered glass trailing. Mount missing. Germany or Venice, early 17th Ct. H. 95 mm. P. London.

Facing page:
292 Flacon. Thick-walled blue glass. Pewter mount and screw lid. France, Orleans, 17/18th Ct. H. 73 mm. C. Schwarzkopf.

293 Flacon, decorated in relief with a pouncing lion and a cross on the reverse. Thick-walled clear glass. Pewter mount. France, Orleans, c. 1680. H. 85 mm. C. Schwarzkopf.

294 Flacons. Clear glass with spiralling red and blue threads. Gold mounts. Spain, La Granja, 18th Ct. H. 86 mm. C. Schwarzkopf.

291 Multi-purpose flacons of flattened pear-shape, all with foot. Two (l. and r.) with inserted boxes closed by push-on lids (these often made from silver coins), and with a tiny pomander on the top. The flacon on the left with its original etui with hand-written dedication of 1691. All clear glass. Silver mounts. Cloudiness of the interior surface (r) indicates the use of these flacons as smelling bottles. England, late 17th Ct. H. 80 mm. P. London.
▷

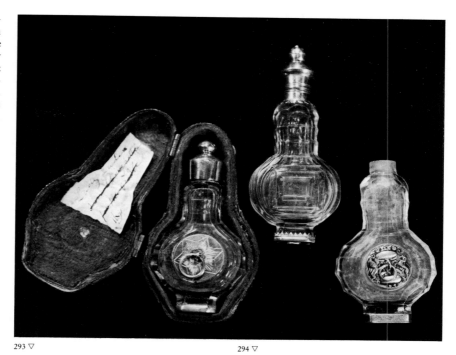

292 ▽

293 ▽

294 ▽

◁◁ 295 Wide-necked flacon with facet-cut spherical body. Glass. Schwarzlot decoration of hunting scene and stylised foliage. Germany. 1st h. 18th Ct. H. 145 mm. KGMC

◁ 296 Almost cylindrical flacon. Clear glass, painted in enamel colours with birds and flowers. Venice, early 18th Ct. H. 90 mm. P. Frankfurt.

◁◁ 297 Flacon. Clear glass cut and engraved with garlands of flowers. Silver mount. Cork stopper with silver top. Bohemia, c. 1740. H. 150 mm. C. Schwarzkopf.

◁ 298 Flacon. Cut thick-walled clear glass, painted in enamel colours with representation of a gardener holding a cactus. Germany, 2nd h. 18th Ct. H. 140 mm. C. Schwarzkopf.

299 Perfume horn. Cut crystal glass. Gold
mounts and chain. France, Semur (?) marked
"AG", c. 1770. L. 80 mm. C. Schwarzkopf. ▷

300 Flacon. Clear glass, cut all over with
shallow facets. Partially covered with gold
cagework. England, 1770/80. H. 75 mm. –
The gold repoussé cap with a white enamel
ribbon and the inscription "L'AMITIE VOUS
L'OFFRE". C. Schwarzkopf.

301 Flacon. Clear crystal glass, cut with
loops and roses. Silver mounts with basket-
like patterns. A pipette, with silver button is
inserted through the shoulder of the flacon.
France, c. 1820. H. 95 mm. C. Schwarzkopf.

302 Gold mounted glass flacon of flattened
tear-shape. France, goldsmith mark Jacques
Meyboon, and Paris discharge mark of
1732–1738. France, 1st h. 18th Ct. Sotheby &
Co.

300 ▽

301 ▽

302 ▽

303 △   306 ▽

305 △

304 △   307 ▽

305

303 Broad-shouldered flacon. Cobalt blue glass. Gilt with a Chinese inspired decoration. England, London (workshop of James Giles) 1770/75. H. 42 mm. P. London.

304 Flacon. White facet-cut glass with decoration in enamel colours. Gold repoussé cap. England, c. 1770–75. H. 46 mm. – On the reverse a small pagoda with bells. MKG/CB

305 Opaque-white glass flacon shallowly cut along the edges. Gilt with an exotic bird in a parkscape. Gold cap over glass stopper. England, London (workshop of James Giles) 1770–1775. H. 72 mm. P. London.

306 Flacon in the shape of a pilgrim's flask, cut with hollow diamond facets and painted in enamel with a duck on a pond and a flying bird. Cobalt blue glass. England, London (Workshop of James Giles), 1770–1775. H. 72 mm. P. London.

307 Flacon. Cobalt blue glass. Gilt with a classical vase surrounded by birds, and with the initials H. W. England, London (probably workshop of James Giles), 1770–1775. H. 100 mm. P. London.

308 Engraved flat elliptical shaped glacon (the engraving also gilt) with flower motifs and the owner's initials. On the reverse there is a rhombic panel of hollow diamonds. Silver push-on cap over glass stopper. Ireland, Waterford, 1790–1800. H. 100 mm. P. London.

309 Flacon in the shape of a pilgrim's flask. Thick-walled glass, cut in steps. "Zwischengold" inset medallion depicting pouncing lion on a red background. Silver mount. Lower Austria, Guttenbrunn, J.J. Mildner, c. 1880. H. 90 mm. P. Munich. ▷

310 Flacon with wheel-engraved relief portrait of William IV. England, London (Apsley Pellat & Co.) 2nd qu. 19th Ct. H. 100 mm. P. Hastings.

311 Flacon with sulphide head of Minerva. Glass elaborately cut. Copper-gilt mount. France, Paris, c. 1820. H. 75 mm. MKG.

312 Flacon, similar to above with sulphide inclusion of two clasped hands. Mushroom-shaped glass stopper. England, London (Apsley Pellat & Co.) 2nd qu. 19th Ct. H. 100 mm. P. London.

Facing page:
313 Flacon cum telescope. Cut clear glass. Mounts brass. Northern Bohemia, c. 1830. H. 53 mm. C. Schwarzkopf.

314 Flacons. Cut clear glass with silver mounts. Bohemia, mid 19th Ct. C. Schwarzkopf.

315 Flacon in the shape of a sea creature. Clear glass with white spiralling stripes. Gold mount and gold mounted cork stopper with small chain. With inscription on blue enamel band "L'amitié plus doux que la rose". England, early 19th Ct. H. 100 mm. C. Schwarzkopf.

316 Cubic flacon. Clear glass with yellow overlay and the engraved symbols of Faith, Love and Hope. Silver mount with forest animals in high relief. Bohemia, c. 1830. H. 95 mm. C. Schwarzkopf.

313 △

315 ▽

314 △

316 ▽

317 Left: Flacon in the shape of a carafe. Thick glass with gold mounts. Netherlands, Amsterdam, Maker W. J. Stekelenburg 1870 to 1890. H. 122 mm. – Right: Similar flacon with silver mounts. Netherlands, late 19th Ct. H. 132 mm. C. Schwarzkopf.

318 Tear-shaped flattened flacons. Clear cut glass with openwork gold mounts and hinged lids. Netherlands, 2nd h. 19th Ct. H. 125 mm. C. Schwarzkopf.

◁ 319 Perfume horn cum vinaigrette. Cut ruby-red glass with silver mounts, hinged repoussé silver cap, chain and suspensory ring. England, mid 19th Ct. L. 70 mm. C. Schwarzkopf.

320 Tear-shaped flattened flacon. Clear cut glass with openwork silver mounts, marked "LB". France, late 19th Ct. H. 120 mm. C. Schwarzkopf.

321 Four-part perfume bottles in clear pressed glass with cut glass stoppers in a copper gilt basket-like mount which is embellished with laurel sprays and rams' heads in high relief. France, 2nd h. 19th Ct. H. 125 mm. C. Schwarzkopf. ▷

322 △

324 ▽

323 △

325 ▽

Facing page:

322 Necessaire in form of a grand piano with a mixing set for perfume of glass and silver, needlework tools of ivory with inlaid mother-of-pearl, a silver eye bowl, writing utensils and a seal. Wooden box with bronze ornaments and a mirror inside the lid. France, Paris, c. 1810. H. 190 mm. C. Schwarzkopf.

323 Standing flacon. Green cut glass. Silver-gilt mounts, hinged repoussé silver cap. France (?) c. 1850/60. H. 107 mm. C. Schwarzkopf.

324 Standing flacon with a circular base. Cut clear glass. Silver-gilt mount with six finely chiselled ornamental fields. Suspensory ring engraved, on a short chain. Glass stopper underneath hinged cap. France, c. 1860/70. H. 57 mm. C. Schwarzkopf.

325 Circular standing flacon. Clear glass. Gold mounts with decoration of dots and meanders. Netherlands, 2nd h. 19th Ct. H. 92 mm. C. Schwarzkopf.

326 △   327 △   328 ▽

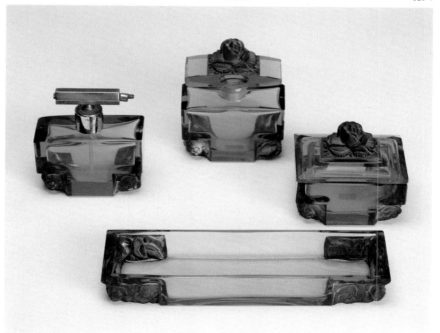

326 Standing flacon for the toilet table. Glass, overlaid with a landscape motif. Sprays of clover leaves in relief and painted gold and black. Silver repoussé screw cap. France, Nancy (Daum Frères), c. 1900 H. 140 mm. C. Schwarzkopf.

327 Table flacon with pineapple-like surface decoration. Matted glass. France, 1920's. H. 170 mm. C. Schwarzkopf.

328 Toilet set. Atomiser, flacon, lidded box and tray. Crystal glass with cut greyish rose motifs. France, Paris, c. 1925. H. 96, 120, 90, 225 mm. C. Schwarzkopf.

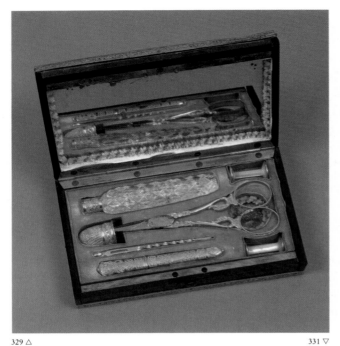

329 △

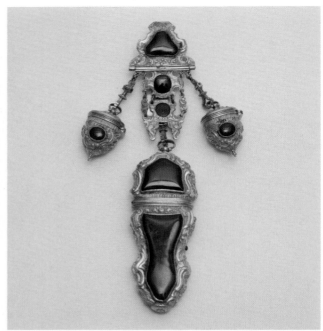

331 ▽

330 △

332 ▽

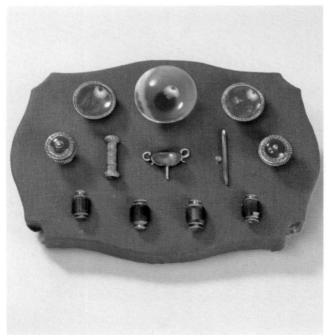

Facing page:

329 Necessaire containing flacon, scissors, thimble, a needle cum ear spoon, etui for sewing needle and two reels of yarn. Cut glass, gold mother-of-pearl. Wooden box with cover of malachite and silver gilt mounts. France, 1810. Etui 124 × 74 × 28 mm, H. flacon 74 mm. C. Schwarzkopf.

330 A lady's chatelaine containing necessaire and two smelling boxes. Copper-gilt with bloodstone. France, 1760. H. 195 mm, boxes 40 mm. – The necessaire comprises ear spoon, pen knife, ivory writing tablet, spoon, needle, pen holder and scissors. C. Schwarzkopf.

331 Perfume and make-up necessaire, with mixing bowl, two lidded boxes, two make-up bowls, a funnel, four small flacons with screw caps, crayon and a miniature telescope. Agate, red ruby glass, silver-gilt mounts. Germany, Augsburg, 1700. D. mixing bowl 58 mm. C. Schwarzkopf.

332 Etui made from a walnut with gold mounts. Two miniature glass flacons and refill funnel. Gold mounts on flacons. England, 1st h. 19th Ct. PG

333 Toilet water flask. Clear and opaque glass with blue overlay, cut. South Germany, 1860/65. H. 135 mm. MKG ▷

334 Mould blown toilet flask in neogothic style. Above a flat ribbed foot stylised foliage in relief within trellis work. Neck ringed. Baldachin-like stopper. Brick-red pressed glass. Frankreich (Launey et Cie), mid 19th Ct. H. 70 mm. P. London.

335 Flacon. Opaque glass, with bevelled edges and ornamented silver cap. Bohemia, c. 1840. H. 75 mm. C. Schwarzkopf.

334 △

335 ▽

◁◁ 336 Flacon of ruby red glass with white glass overlay, with wheelcut foliage motif. Cork stopper with silver mount. Bohemia, c. 1850. H. 23 mm. C. Schwarzkopf.

◁ 337 Flacon. Black glass with flowers in enamel colours. Brass mount. Screw cap and pipette. Bohemia, 2nd h. 19th Ct. H. 65 mm. C. Schwarzkopf.

◁◁ 338 Standing flacon. Milky white glass with applied silver clover leaves. Bohemia, c. 1830/40. H. 138 mm. C. Schwarzkopf.

◁ 339 Atomiser. Milk glass with blue and gold painted flower sprays. Pewter mount, plunger mechanism. Bohemia, late 19th Ct. H. 22 mm. C. Schwarzkopf.

340 Flacon standing on three spherical feet. Clear glass painted with a girl in rural surrounding in "Schwarzlot". Austria, Vienna (J. & L. Lobmeyr), 1860/80. H. 92 mm. C. Schwarzkopf. ▷

341 Flacon in opaque white glass with flat surfaces. Lavishly decorated in enamel colours with birds and flowers. Silver repoussé hinged cap over glass stopper. France, 2nd h. 19th Ct. H. 105 mm. P. London ▷▷

342 Left: Lyra-shaped flacons. Clear glass, cut and painted in red (representation of a deer and flowers). Silver hinged lid. Bohemia, 2nd h. 19th Ct. H. 115 mm – Centre: Similar flacon, decorated in red with a Chinese dancer. Gold hinged cap over glass stopper. Netherlands, 2nd h. 19th Ct. H. 122 mm. – Right: Similar flacon with representation of a dog and horns of plenty in red colour. Silver mount marked "ICK". Bohemia, 2nd h. 19th Ct. H. 115 mm. C. Schwarzkopf ▷

343 Icicle-shaped cologne bottle. Clear glass overlaid with red and skilfully cut to form a spiral ribbon. The intervening surface wheel-engraved with conifer needles and cones. Silver screw cap. England, London 1887. L. 25 mm. C. Schwarzkopf.

344 Left: Smelling bottle of cylindrical shape. Green glass with silver mount and hinged cap. Green glass stone mounted on release button. England, Birmingham, 1897/98. H. 75 mm. – Right: Similar smelling bottle. Ruby red glass with silver mount and hinged cap. Maker's mark "CM". England, Birmingham, 1901/02. H. 83 mm. C. Schwarzkopf.

345 Double flacons with separate chambers for perfume and smelling salts. Red-flashed, clear and green-flashed glass, embellished by cutting in various patterns. Mounts and hinged lids or screw caps, brass, gilt or silver. England, mid to end 19th Ct. L. (f. l. to r.) 157, 125, 109, 130 mm. C. Schwarzkopf.

346, 347 Double flacon in original padded case. Clear glass. Brass mounts. England, 1867. L. 127 mm. – The screw cap of the smelling salt compartment is engraved with "G. W. 1867" and a cross. The flacon is closed by a hinged lid with spring-release mechanism. The engraved "EL" seems to indicate the owner. This double flacon is hinged in the middle between the two compartments in imitation of a pair of opera glasses (Ill. 346). C. Schwarzkopf.

348 Above: Double flacon in its original case. Dark green glass mounted in a cage of silver-gilt, which is embellished with corals. Gilt screw-cap for perfume compartment and patented spring-release cap for the smelling salt section. England, 1872. L. 117 mm. P. London. – Below: Cylindrical double flacon. Green pressed glass. Gunmetal mounts. England, 2nd h. 19th Ct. L. 138 mm. P. Hastings.   ▷

197

349 Pendant flacon. Millifiori glass with av-
enturine effect. Inserted medallion with lion's
head. Brass mount and hinged cap with set
"gem" of facet-cut ruby-red glass. Italy, 2nd
h. 19th Ct. H. 70 mm. C. Schwarzkopf.

350 Flacon in the form of a fish (above) and
of a duck's head (below). Cameo glass, red
glass with grey glass overlay. Silver mounts,
in the fish bottle the caudal fin serves as screw
closure. England, Thomas Webb & Sons, late
19th Ct. L. 95 and 110 mm. P. London.

351 Flacon of circular outline. Ruby-red
glass harnessed with open-work brass mount;
hinged brass cap above glass stopper. England, late 19th Ct. H. 62 mm. C. Schwarzkopf.   ▷

352 Cylindrical flacon. Triple overlay glass,
cut and with gilt painted decoration. Silver-
gilt mount. Maker's mark "W.T.", England,
London 1879/80. H. 110 mm. C. Schwarzkopf.   ▷ ▷

354 Necessaire containing two gold ornamented glass flacons, mirror, needlework implements and toilet utensils, all attached to six wing-like doors which open, accompanied by a tune when the knob on top of the necessaire is turned. Black varnished wood with brass fittings and bronze ornaments. Germany, Feuchtwangen (Black Forest), Lamy & Co., c. 1870. H. 33 mm. C. Schwarzkopf.

◁ 353 Cologne or smelling bottle in cameo glass with opaque white cherry motif on light blue ground. Hinged silver cap over glass stopper. England (Thomas Webb & Sons) c. 1887. H. 105 mm. P. London.

355 △   358 ▽   356 △   359 ▽   357 △   360 ▽

Facing page:

355   Cologne bottle. Matt yellow glass with dark brown overlay, with representation of a cyclamen. Silver metal mount. Stopper missing. Signed "Payadis". France, Nancy, c. 1900. H. 125 mm. C. Schwarzkopf.

356   Atomiser. Clear glass with red and dark-violet surface staining. Brass mount. France, c. 1905. H. 145 mm. C. Schwarzkopf.

357   Atomiser. Ruby red flashed glass. Copper mount incomplete. France, c. 1900. H. 195 mm. C. Schwarzkopf.

358   Sculptural flacon. Glass, thick-walled with deep acid-etched channels and controlled flow air bubbles. France, Maurice Marinot, 1929. H. 162 mm. V. & A.

359   Flacon of thick-walled clear glass, with the arrested flow of air bubbles as decorative element. France, Maurice Marinot, 1931. H. 123 mm. V. & A.

360   Flacon. Overlay of clear coloured glass on pink glass with inclusions. France, Maurice Marinot, c. 1929. H. 95 mm. Collection Funke-Kaiser, Cologne.

361   Art Nouveau flacon. Decoration of water lilies in green and purple overlay on opaque marbled orange-red glass. Silver mount with applied gilt flowers and leaves. France, Nancy (signed on glass "Gallé", on metal "AC" with "trompet") c. 1890. H. 110 mm. KGMC

362   Flacon. Milky glass with brown overlay; orange, rosa and bright green shining spangle. France, Nancy, Emile Gallé, c. 1895. H. 165 mm. C. Schwarzkopf.

361

362

363 △

364 △

365 ▽

366 ▽

367 △   368 ▷

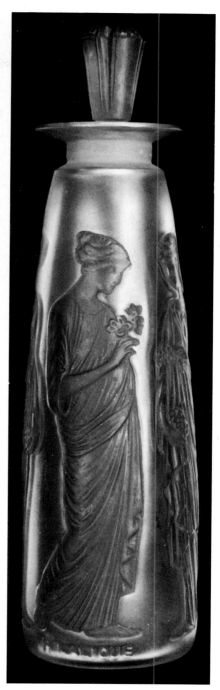

To pages 202 and 203:
363–368 Flacons. Colourless, partly matted glass. All by René Lalique, France. – 363: Flower relief, c. 1970. H. 90 mm. P. Hamburg. – 364: Pendant with two eyelets, acid-etched leaves of Eucalyptus, mushroom stopper, c. 1920. H. 46 mm. PG – 365: Clear glass, ground stopper extended into the flacon taking the form of a thinly veiled female figure. Early 20th Ct. H. 150 mm. P. Frankfurt. – 366: "Hélène" pressed glass, c. 1928. H. 60 mm. Collection Funke-Kaiser, Cologne.–367: Thistle decoration in relief. 1920's. H. 104 mm; "Pearl". 1920's. H. 140 mm; "Sea-urchin" (inscribed on underside "Rotterdam Lloyd, Royal Dutch Mail"). 1920's. H. 95 mm. C. Schwarzkopf – 368: Matt glass with intaglio decoration of Greek-inspired dancers. Early 20th Ct. H. 153 mm. P. Hastings. – For other pieces by R. Lalique see Ill. 32 and 287.

To page 204:
369 Flacon for the toilet table. Cut crystal glass body within a silvered metal stand on four spherical feet, with openwork representing insects. Silver-plated screw cap. Bohemia, 1920's H. 105 mm. C. Schwarzkopf.

370 Flacon. Malachite glass, decorated with sunflowers cut in relief. Glass stopper extended far into the flacon. Northern Bohemia, Kosten, Joseph Rindskopf, c. 1910/20. H. 142 mm. C. Schwarzkopf.

371 Toilet set, comprising one flacon and two atomisers. Colourless crystal glass with engraved birds and flowers; gilt areas with irregular decoration by acid-etching. Czechoslovakia, Karlsbad, Moser, 1920's. H. (f. l. to r.) 130, 110, 250 mm. C. Schwarzkopf.

372 Atomiser and flacon. Colourless cut lead-crystal glass flashed black and wheel engraved with flowers. Metal mount. Germany, Fachschule Cologne, 1930's. H. 110 mm and 165 mm. C. Schwarzkopf.

369 △

371 ▽   370 △

372 ▽

Acknowledgments

I am grateful for the assistance afforded to me in my work on this book by the directors and members of staff of many of our European museums, by private collectors and countless other people. My special thanks for their advice and support go to Dr. and Mrs. J. Godfrey and Gillian Godfrey, Leeds; Dr. D. Furniss, Leeds; Mr. H. E. Frost, Worcester; Mr. P. Green, Littlehampton; Mr. R. G. Thomas, Southampton; Miss W. Evans, London; Miss. E. Dawson, London; Mr. J. V. G. Mallet, London; Mr. R. J. Charleston, Richmond, Surrey; Mr. A. Chater, Richmond, Surrey; Victor Launert, Richmond, Surrey; Frau G. Funke-Kaiser, Cologne; Dr. Gisela Reineking von Bock, Cologne; Dr. I. Krummer-Schrot, Freiburg i. Br.; Prof. R. Becksmann, Freiburg i. Br.; Prof. A. Dreier, Berlin; Dr. H. Roessler, Munich; Dr. H. H. Heine, Paris; and Frau E. Münzing, Munich.

I am particularly indebted to Mrs. I. Vijt den Bogaard and Mr. G. H. Garnman, Amsterdam, for the spontaneous enthusiasm they showed for this project; their contribution was invaluable.

Thanks also to Mrs. M. Tebbs and Miss. C. Davey, both of London, for the execution of the line drawings, and to the photographers working either in the museum service or at the behest of private collectors who have brought their skill to bear in the photographing of the objects. Pamela Leighton and Celia Bradley who produced immaculate typescript of the English translation deserve my gratitude.

Special mention must be made of Herr Kai Falck, the Schwarzkopf Company photographer, who is responsible for most of the photographs of his firm's collection and for many of specimens from the Museum für Kunst und Gewerbe, Hamburg.

It is difficult to find adequate words to thank two people in particular: Frau Maria Jedding-Gesterling, Curator of the Schwarzkopf Collection at Steinhorst for her painstaking surveillance in the work of supplying information for the captions for objects in her care, and Herr Dr. Hermann Jedding of the Museum für Kunst und Gewerbe, Hamburg, for the generous way in which he made available material from the rich store of his museum.

Last but not least, warmest thanks to Herr Dr. Karl Josef Ballhaus, director of Hans Schwarzkopf GmbH, for the generous support lent to this project, without which it would not have seen the light of day.

Richmond, Surrey, Autumn 1987   Edmund Launert

Bibliography

Angeloglou, M., A History of Make-up, London 1970

Barbe, S., Le Parfumeur François, 4. Aufl., Paris 1668

Barrelet, J., La Verrerie en France, Paris 1953

Bayle, V., L'Amateur de Parfums, Grasse 1953

Beard, G., Nineteenth Century Cameo Glass, Newport 1956

Bock, Gisela Reineking von, Bäder, Duft und Seife, Kulturgeschichte der Hygiene, Ausstellungskatalog, Kunstgewerbemuseum Köln 1976

Boehn, M. von, Das Beiwerk der Mode, München 1928

Chapman, H. W., The last Tudor King, London 1961

Corbin, A., Le Miasme et la Jonquille. L'odorat et l'imaginaire social XVIIIᵉ–XIXᵉ siècles, Paris 1982

Delieb, E., Silver boxes, London 1968

Dölger, F. G., Der heilige Fisch in den antiken Religionen, Münster 1922

Ferguson, J., Bibliotheca chemica, London 1954

Foster, K., Scent bottles, London 1966

Friedrich, F., Symbolik der mosaischen Stiftshütte, Leipzig 1841

Hansmann, L., u. Kriss-Rettenbeck, L., Amulett und Talisman, München 1966

Heitmann, B., Die deutschen sogenannten Reiseservice und die Toilettengarnituren von 1680 bis zum Ende des Rokoko. Diss. Univ. München/ Hamburg 1979

Hibbott, H. W., Handbook of Cosmetic Science, London 1963

Honey, W. B., The Art of the Potter, London 1946

Hughes, Th., More small decorative antiques, London 1962

Jackson, Sir Ch., An illustrated history of English plate, 2 Bde., London 1911

Jedding, H., Porzellan aus der Sammlung Blohm, Große Bilderhefte I, Museum für Kunst und Gewerbe, Hamburg 1968

Jokelson, P., Sulphides, London 1968

Kelly, A., Decorative Wedgwood in Architecture and Furniture, London 1965

Latham, R., u. Matthews, W., The Diary of Samuel Pepys, London 1970

Launert, E., Scent & Scent bottles, London 1974

Löw, I., Die Flora der Juden, Bd. IV, Hildesheim 1967

Mankowitz, W., Wedgwood, London 1966

Matthews, L. G., The Antiques of Perfume, London 1973

Morley-Fletcher, H., Meißen, London 1970

Naves, Y. R., u. Mazuer, G., Les parfums naturels, Paris 1939

Patzaurek, G., Die Gläser der Empire- und Biedermeierzeit, Leipzig 1923

Percy, V., The Glass of Lalique, London 1977

Piesse, S. G. W., The art of perfumery, 4. Aufl., London 1879

Piesse, S. G. W., Histoire des parfums, Paris 1905

Piesse, S. G. W., Chimie des parfums, Paris 1917

Rimmel, E., The Book of Perfumes, London 1865

Schlosser, J. von, Die Kunst- und Wunderkammern der Spätrenaissance, Leipzig 1908

Smollich, R., Der Bisamapfel in Kunst und Wissenschaft, Stuttgart 1983

Thompson, C. J. S., The Mystery and Lure of Perfume, London 1927

Walcha, O., Meißener Porzellan, Dresden 1973

Articles

Charleston, R.J., James Giles as a decorator of glass, The Connoisseur, Juni/Juli 1966

Charleston, R.J., Battersea, Bilston or Birmingham? Victoria & Albert Museum Bulletin No. 3, S. 1–44 (1967)

Charleston, R.J., The Glass of Maurice Marinot, Victoria & Albert Museum Bulletin No. 1, S. 1–8 (1965)

De Coo, J., Vom Bettelmönch zum Riechfläschchen, Pantheon 1984

Ladendorf, H., Der Duft und die Kunstgeschichte, Festschr. E. Mayer, Hamburg 1957

Lane, A., u. Charleston, R.J., Girl in a Swing porcelain and Chelsea?, English Ceramic Circle, Transactions 1962

Launert, E., Scent and Scent Bottles, Collector's Guide, August/September 1971

Paumier, Ch., Une exposition d'Art décoratif à 18 Hôtel de la Revue Les Arts, Les Arts 150 (1914)

Pichter, E., Riechschnecke als Pestschutzamulett, Deutsche Gaue 1952

Polak, A., Sulphides and Medals, Journal of Glass Studies No. 8 (1966)

Spiegel, W., Parfumflakons der Biedermeierzeit, Weltkunst Nr. 5,6 (1984)

Tate, H., An anonymous loan to the British Museum of Renaissance jewellery, The Connoisseur, November 1963

Vailat, L., Marinot, Peintre Verrier, L'Art et les Artistes 19 (1914)

Wenham, E., Pomanders, The Connoisseur, April 1934

Index

Bold figures indicate text figures or illustrations